HUMANISING ARTIFICIAL INTELLIGENCE

Navigating Human-Machine Collaborations in the Age of Disruption

Femi Stevens

HUMANITY AND TECHNOLOGY SERIES

HUMANISING ARTIFICIAL INTELLIGENCE

Navigating Human-Machine Collaborations in the Age of Disruption

Published by New Generation Publishing in 2024

First Edition

Paperback ISBN: 9-781-83563-166-9
eBook ISBN: 9-781-83563-167-6

www.newgeneration-publishing.com

To the explorers who dream and believe in a new world yet unseen

Yemi, Michelle, Royal, Mabel;

Josh and Grace

Thank you for your unfailing support and faith.

ACKNOWLEDGMENTS

There are so many people who deserve recognition and thanks for this work that I could fill several volumes with names alone. I want to personally thank everyone who shared in the formation of the ideas presented here, and to the ones reading this, may you find intellectual virtues and enlightenment contained within the pages of this book.

My thanks go out to the entire team at GM Artificial Intelligence (AI) Foundry, UK; the Centre for Digital Innovation, UK; The Alan Turin Institute (ATI), UK; the faculty, and staff at Manchester Metropolitan University and The University of Manchester, UK, where the Humanising Artificial Intelligence (HAI) project took its first breath of inspiration. In particular, I want to express my gratitude to distinguished professors and erudites in the persons of Darren Dancey, Keeley Crockett, Rob Aspin, Bamidele Adebisi, Simon Reeve, Gbenga Olumodimu, Ismail Adeniran, Sunday Ekpo, Segun Popoola, Olamide Jogunola, Hamad S. Alromaih, Peter Smith, Micheal Dobson, Effa Ettah, and many families and friends for their encouragement and support.

Contents

FOREWORD

Thousands of years of human history have seen technological advancements from basic stone tools to intricate automation, digital technology, and genetic engineering like nanobiotechnology. The first self-moving machine in Greek mythology was Talos, a huge bronze automaton made by Hephaestus, the god of invention and blacksmithing. Talos was built at the request of the god Zeus as a protector from invaders for the island of Crete, where his lover Europa lived. Thus, the story of Talos, first mentioned around 700 B.C. by Hesiod, offers one of the earliest conceptions of a robot and artificial life.[i][ii]

Alan Turing's 1950 paper "Computing Machinery and Intelligence" introduced the concept of artificial intelligence (AI). This was years before the community adopted the term Artificial Intelligence, as coined by John McCarthy. This concept and recent studies pose the simple question, "Can machines think?"[iii][iv]

Turing then proposed a method for evaluating whether machines can think, which came to be known as the Turing test. The test, or "Imitation Game" as it was called in the paper, was put forth as a simple test that could prove that machines could think. The Turing test takes a simple, pragmatic approach, assuming that a computer that is indistinguishable from an intelligent human has shown that machines can think.[iv]

To understand the future of technology, we need to study the history of AI. Efforts have been made to collect, preserve, analyse, and interpret this history. The dynamic and ever-growing nature of this field makes this book both challenging and critical. Every aspect of Humanising Artificial Intelligence (HAI) as a model was subjected to rigorous reviews and several attempts to ensure far-reaching representation with inputs from influential research, experience, and evidence-based products. Also, the topical area and structure are produced to fill the knowledge gap across socio-cultural and political spheres and to serve as a bridge between the principles and practices of ethics, trustworthiness, and governance of AI and data management as they affect humanity and the planet.

There have been exciting advancements in AI and its governance with human oversight and control. However, the release of Open AI's generative AIs (GPT – generative pre-trained transformers) has prompted a mixed flurry of excitement and apprehension. The widespread fascination with GPT "suggests a potential mindless path to artificial general and superintelligence." Radical innovations in AI applications have accelerated the evolution of development towards a total revolution of AI systems roadmap from specialises in one area solving one problem (Artificial Narrow Intelligence (ANI)) to AI that is as smart as a human in many aspects (Artificial General Intelligence (AGI)) and to conscious AI-based system that surpasses human capabilities and more intelligent than human brains in all fields (Artificial Super Intelligence (ASI)).[iv] Moreover, the invention of ASI is considered a hypothesis of technological singularity, also known as the singularity, which will usher in advancements and transformations that are profound, rapid, and unfathomable to human civilisation. Consequently, the HAI book's thrust is to proactively inspire, educate, facilitate, and support multidiscipline and multicultural collaborations in humanising[v] all aspects of AI innovations by instituting and incorporating wide-ranging human values, trustworthy standards and ethos into the design, development, deployment, and decommissioning of AI applications for the good of people and planet.

HUMANISING ARTIFICIAL INTELLIGENCE

Navigating Human-Machine Collaborations in the Age of Disruption

REFLECTION: AI AND FUTURE OF INTELLIGENCE

"I am ChatGPT. ... My main goal is to be a useful tool for people looking for information. I strive to provide accurate and helpful answers as best I can be based on my programming and training. ... I have no personal goals or motivations, as I am an artificial intelligence and have no consciousness or emotions. ... Inside me, I analyse the input I receive, break it down into its parts, and use algorithms to generate an answer based on the patterns and relationships I have learned from my training data. ... My training data consists of much text from various sources, such as books, articles, and websites"

— ChatGPT ("Answer to prompts" August 4, 2023. Reference Chapter 3/No. 19)

Personal Note:

1

THE FUTURE OF INTELLIGENCE

The New Earthly Oil and Gold

The world's most valuable resource in this era is neither oil nor gold. Knowledge as a combination of information and data is critical in socio-economic production and distribution in the global playground. The knowledge-based economy, which can also be regarded as the digital economy, is a system in which demand, production, and distribution of goods and services are knowledge-driven and expert-based. Tangible contributions are decreasing as things become more digital. Human capital and intellectual property are vital for the survival of people, the planet, and businesses, and we build all these with digital capital and intelligence.

In this digital economy, constant and rapid advances in technology and innovation, especially in artificial intelligence and data management, present enormous opportunities for human development and social good. However, with these vast opportunities come issues and potential threats to human life, well-being, autonomy, and society. The severe issues and potential risks surrounding AI applications are centred on their trustworthiness. This is explained by overarching principles of fairness, transparency, and accountability of their lifecycle, including conceptualisation, design, development, deployment, and use, and as they affect individuals, governmental organisations, non-governmental organisations, and society.

Because of errors and biases, AI applications have limitations, risks, and issues. It is well known that AI algorithms, data

3

collection, and data processing have a probabilistic guarantee of accuracy when dealing with structured and unstructured datasets. Coupled with intentional and unintentional biases, these are what make up the multifaceted ethical and governance issues that this book is written to address.

The Race Among Nations and Global Digital Supremacy

Economic and political gains are the driving force behind the global race for artificial intelligence supremacy. This has also led to social and cultural needs related to human and societal requirements. Using a responsible and sustainable approach to designing, developing, deploying, and decommissioning AI applications that prioritise social good instead of profit and social control is essential.

The trends in the race for global superpower in AI show significant players such as the US, China, the UK, and countries of continental Europe having different approaches to the end-to-end governance of AI and data management. However, Europe has the advantage of more robust environmental management practices and legal frameworks for data protection, which have inspired other parts of the world. This can facilitate its drive towards global leadership in the research and use of AI and other emerging technologies.[1]

Among these regions or countries, China is on its way to becoming the first global superpower for Artificial Intelligence based on her ambitious AI strategy that is built on a massive amount of data, talents, AI companies, and capital to build the world's leading AI ecosystem. [2]

The USA has arguably exhibited leadership traits in the early years of the evolution of AI. However, its global influence has declined in recent years compared to China, Europe, and the UK. People have debated, legislated, and researched how to make AI ethical as it becomes increasingly prevalent. Artificial Intelligence can imitate and reproduce human intelligence in various tasks for better outcomes. As computing systems, they can also, by extension, deliver different services or find applications in different areas of human endeavour and enterprise, such as natural language processing, speech recognition, machine vision, and knowledge-based and expert systems.

The Scale and Scope of Artificial Intelligence Applications

The adoption, application, and use of AI would increase with the attendant creation of new sets of job, leadership, and management skills. This is even more feasible as the world yearns for greater productivity, affordability, personalisation, increased capability, and better quality of life across different industries and sectors such as retail, healthcare, automotive, financial services, agriculture, technology, communication, entertainment, government, etc. Based on ongoing research and projections in the market, the primary source of disruption, transformation, and competitive advantage would be AI-based solutions, which would serve as critical enablers to create and maximise opportunities and strengths and minimise and eliminate threats and weaknesses.

We cannot quantify the global market of Artificial Intelligence and its impact on every facet of life, both now and in the foreseeable future. However, for necessity and proportionality, the statistics provided in this book are with a margin of tolerance regarding the actual status and offer perspectives on how principles and practices that are based on linear models do not manage exponential growth and tackle the existential threats that these "inorganic intelligent lives" portend for humanity.

The current global market of AI is driven more by the need for greater productivity, and it is set to potentially contribute $15.7tr by 2030 to the global economy, offering up to 26% boost in GDP for local economies, approximately 300 use cases identified in impact index. [3]

Artificial Intelligence: Meaning, Types and Trends

The term artificial intelligence (AI) was first coined by John McCarthy in 1956 when he held the first academic conference on the subject.[4] The journey to understand whether machines can truly think began before that. Artificial intelligence (AI) is shaping the future of technology and innovation, which, by extension, influences and affects our lives. But what is AI? According to studies, experiments, and the use of AI in different industries and sectors, AI is understood in different domains as a machine's ability to display human-like capabilities such as reasoning, learning, planning, and creativity.[5]

AI is a machine's ability to perform the cognitive (intellectual) functions we associate with human minds, such as perceiving, reasoning, learning, interacting with an environment, problem-solving, and even exercising creativity. [6]

Artificial intelligence (AI) is the ability of a digital computer or computer-controlled robot to perform tasks commonly associated with intelligent beings. [7]

Since the development and use of the digital computer in the 1940s, it has been demonstrated that computers can be programmed to carry out various complex tasks—such as discovering proofs for mathematical theorems or playing chess — with excellent proficiency. Despite continuing advances in computer processing speed and memory capacity, there are yet no programs that can match complete human flexibility over broader domains or in tasks requiring much of everyday knowledge and skillsets. Some programs[7] have attained the performance levels of human experts and professionals in performing certain specific tasks, so artificial intelligence in this limited sense is found in applications as diverse as medical diagnosis, computer search engines, voice or handwriting recognition, chatbots, etc

AI works as technical systems that learn from their environment by gathering data from their sensors and from data input by humans, processing and analysing the data and responding by acting to achieve a specific goal and solve problems. Also, AI systems can adapt their behaviour to a certain degree by analysing the effects of previous actions and working autonomously. AI technology is widely used throughout industry, government, and science. [8] Some high-profile applications of AI and major domains are as follows:

- advanced web search engines, e.g., Google Search, Microsoft Bing

- recommendation systems used, e.g., YouTube, Amazon, Netflix

- understanding human speech, e.g., Siri and Alexa

- self-driving cars, e.g., Waymo,

- generative AI or creative tools, e.g., ChatGPT, AI art

- competing at the highest level in strategic games, e.g., AlphaGo, IBM Watson

- expert system, e.g., DoNotPay (world's first robot lawyer [8])

- computer vision, e.g., Yolo, Google Translate, Sentioscope, etc.

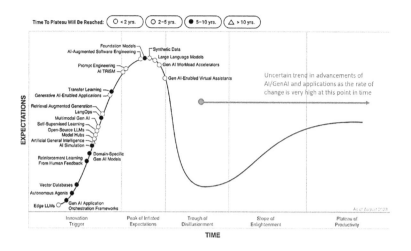

Figure 1.1: The Gartner Hype Cycle for AI/GenAI

- The above graphic representation and trend of the maturity and adoption of AI/GenAI technologies and applications, and how they will evolve with time and potential relevance to solving real business problems and exploiting new opportunities (Gartner Hype Cycle[1]).

Classifications and Types of Artificial Intelligence

"We have a very good idea of sort of roughly what (AI) is doing. But as soon as it gets really complicated, we don't actually know what's going on any more than we know what's going on in your brain…we designed the learning algorithm…But when this learning algorithm then interacts with data, it produces complicated neural networks that are good at doing things. But we don't really understand exactly how they do those things…one of the ways in which these systems might escape control is by writing their own computer code to modify

9

themselves. And that's something we need to seriously worry about" - Geoffrey HintonQ2 ('Godfather of AI')

AI-based applications are evolving and are broadly categorised based on their purposes and functionalities. Based on the performance levels of different AI applications, AI can be divided into two categories: Strong Artificial Intelligence and Weak Artificial Intelligence. Whereas strong AI, with examples like self-driving vehicles and sci-fi-movies called The Terminator, has a greater scope of tasks and applications, higher human-level intelligence, and uses unsupervised and reinforced learning modes of data processing whilst weak AI, with examples like recommender systems (chatbots), this has a narrow scope of task and application, it is deployed to solve a specific problem and relied on supervised and semi-supervised learning mode of data processing.

Moreover, AI can be classified into types based on their purposes and impact on human civilisation, namely Artificial Narrow Intelligence (ANI), Artificial General Intelligence (AGI), and Artificial Super Intelligence (ASI). Currently, ANI is the most common in the market; they have narrow capabilities functioning in specific contexts like recommending products on e-commerce platforms or for weather forecasts. AGI is theoretical, exhibiting human-level cognitive functions and capacities like reasoning, thinking, language, and image processing, whilst ASI is more in a science-fiction territory; ASI, as a radical progression from AGI, could surpass all human capabilities. This would include decision-making, rational decisions, and things like making better art and building emotional relationships.[9]

Global Trends and Forecasts

The global survey and discovery of AI's most impactful innovations and applications show the growth and influence on various industries and sectors, the economy, and the workforce. From productivity, customer engagement, market-size projections, etc., the trends and analyses provide a glimpse of the understanding of AI's rapid evolution and potential to shape the future of business, technology, and human existence in the coming years as shown below in a report based on PWC/Forbes Advisor survey. [10]

❖ **Global Economy**

AI could contribute up to $15.7 trillion to the global economy in 2030, more than the current output of China and India combined. Of this, $6.6 trillion is likely to come from increased productivity, and $9.1 trillion is expected to come from consumption-side effects. Also, the most significant gains from AI will likely be in China (a boost of up to 26% of GDP in 2030) and North America (a potential 14% boost). The most significant sector gains will be in retail, financial services, and healthcare, as AI increases productivity, product quality, and consumption. (PwC report) [10]

❖ **Business Productivity**

Over 60% of business owners believe AI will increase productivity. Specifically, 64% stated that AI would

---

improve business productivity, and 42% thought it would streamline job processes. 64% of business owners believe AI has the potential to improve customer relationships, showing a positive outlook on the role of AI in enhancing client interactions. As reported by Grand View Research, AI continues to revolutionise various industries, with an expected annual growth rate of 37.3% between 2023 and 2030. This shows the growing confidence in AI's potential to transform business operations.

❖ Labour and Employability

As AI develops, it could displace 400 million workers worldwide. A McKinsey report predicts that between 2016 and 2030, AI-related advancements may affect 15% of the global workforce. As labour shortages become a pressing concern, 25% of companies are adopting AI to address this issue, according to an IBM report. AI helps businesses optimise operations and compensates for the lack of human resources. According to World Economic Forum research, we project AI to create around 97 million new jobs, potentially countering workforce displacement concerns. [10]

❖ Customer Experience

54% believe AI can enhance long-form written content, such as website content. Instant messaging, including chatbots, was a potential area for improvement by 53% of participants, while 46% thought text messages and 48% considered emails could benefit from AI integration. Furthermore, 39% of consumers felt AI could improve phone calls, and 40% saw potential in personalised advertising. 37% of respondents identified personalised services, such as product recommendations, as an area where AI could make a positive impact. However, 5% were unsure about AI's role in enhancing customer experience, and 8% didn't think AI could improve anything. [10]

❖ Usage and Adoption by Consumers

The survey shows how consumers plan to incorporate AI into their everyday activities. Results reveal that people are interested in using AI to assist with tasks such as replying to texts or emails from friends and colleagues (45%), finding answers to financial questions (43%) and putting together travel itineraries (38%). AI is viewed as a helpful resource for writing emails (31%), getting ready for job interviews (30%), creating social media posts (25%), and breaking down complex or lengthy information (19%). While 6% of the respondents were uncertain about how they might use AI, 11% expressed that they were not inclined to use AI for any reason.[10]

❖ Misinformation and Mistrust

Misinformation and mistrust are significant concerns for consumers regarding AI implementation in businesses. According to the survey data, 76% of respondents express concern about AI causing misinformation on a business's website, with 43% being very concerned and 33% somewhat concerned. On the other hand, 14% remain neutral, neither concerned nor unconcerned about the possibility of AI-induced misinformation. Only a small percentage, 4% and 5% are unconcerned or very unconcerned, respectively.[10]

More detail is discussed in the case study section of this book, covering an in depth analysis of the Social, Moral, Cultural, Environmental, Legal, Economic, Political, and Ethical Issues of AI-based Facial Recognition Technology (FRT).

❖ Bias and Discrimination

Some common occurrences are as follows – For data-related bias and discrimination cases, researchers in information sciences find bias in up to 38.6% of 'facts' used by AI.[11] Those biases were both positive and negative. Studies cover different groups from categories like religion, gender, race, and profession to see if the data was favouring or disfavouring them, and it was discovered that there are severe cases of prejudice and biases. Muslims are associated with words like terrorism, Mexicans with poverty, police officers with death, priests with paedophilia, and lawyers with dishonesty. Performing artists, politicians, detectives, pharmacists, and handypersons are discriminated against. [18] [19]

For AI model and algorithm bias cases, researchers in diagnostic imaging and meta-analysis find a high risk of bias in 83% of AI neuroimaging models for psychiatric diagnosis. They analysed 555 AI models for detecting psychiatric disorders from 517 studies and assessed their quality and risk of bias. Out of 555 AI models, the researchers used PROBAST and CLEAR systems to find that 461 models (83.1%) had high ROB. It was also noted that there are inadequate sample sizes in 71.7 per cent (398 models) and insufficient handling of data complexity in 99.1 per cent (550 models) of the AL models. [12]

More detail is discussed in the case study section of this book, covering an in-depth analysis of the Social, Moral, Cultural, Environmental, Legal, Economic, Political, and Ethical Issues of AI-based Facial Recognition Technology (FRT).

Welcome The Age of Hyperpowers and Uberpowers

Throughout history, there has never been a single global international system and truly supreme leader. What had existed are regional leaders and countries that have fluctuated in terms of exercising extensive political and economic control. But it was not until after the Cold War that any country or continent possessed the power of life and death over the entire planet. During the Cold War, there were two such powers. The need to avoid a nuclear confrontation between the two superpowers turned the Cold War into an ideological war. The US and the Soviet Union dominated the world politically and economically to an extent never seen. When the Soviet Union collapsed, all that power passed to the United States—and the world's first Hyperpower was born. Hyperpower became the new term which captured America's role as the only superpower in the world because it cannot be limited by a commensurate opposing force.[13]

These crucial findings come from the Global Power Index 2023 and have been supported by the Asia Power Index since 2018. The aim, quantitative and wholistic measure of power and influence, and the future forecast of distribution and balance of power entirely among countries and regions show that the United States still has the lead on the military capacity, cultural influence, resilience, and defence networks, but falls behind China in economic and future resources, economic relationships, and diplomatic influence. Although people still argue that the United Kingdom is the only country ever to be a Hyperpower because of the size of its Empire (the biggest in history), the problems facing the world today are borderless beyond politics, economics, science, culture, and military power. They require a leader who possesses both hard and soft powers combined with the legitimacy of a truly universal power. To have universal legitimacy, a power must show it has solutions for the world's problems. Such a power would be more than a superpower or Hyperpower—it would be an Uberpower.

The future of intelligence and global power will depend on an entity with advanced communication and media capabilities. This entity will learn and analyse everything, communicate with anyone regardless of language or culture, and control the communication of other entities, both friendly and hostile.[14] Tech giants, media, governments, and social media were accused of hiding information during COVID-19 and the 2019 US election. Evidence suggests that advanced technology companies and super-intelligent AI will collaborate in the knowledge economy. The fight for power in digital capitalism and dictatorship will pit technology companies against political entities and civil societies.

The Rise of Moral Machines and Superintelligence

Uberpower will soon combine several advanced technologies, including AI, blockchain, and virtual realities, with socio-political ideology and synthetic biological material. Many partly regard this as the singularity of a hypothetical future where technology growth is irreversible and out of control, like an Uberpower with superhuman-level intelligence, capability, and influence to radically and unpredictably transform our livelihoods and reality.

16

The looming intelligence explosion would extensively and radically impact human civilisation, erasing all socio-geographical, cultural, language and religious boundaries by showing capabilities and capacities that transcend human intelligence and capacity. A known catalyst is the intersection between human and computer interfaces and programming via genetic engineering, brain implants, etc. This section discusses Artificial General Intelligence (AGI), which can do things beyond human abilities, such as consciousness and common sense.

The multi-dimensional risks and threats inherent in the rampant rise of AI-based applications and their interaction with humans are enormous if concerted and calculated, and collaboration efforts are not in place on multi-disciplinary, multi-national, and multi-cultural levels to address and mitigate them proactively. Research communities are shocked at the wonders of Chat Generative Pretrained Transformers (ChatGPT) 'smartness' in finding solutions to puzzles like how to stably stack a book, nine eggs, a laptop, a bottle, and a nail. Another study suggested that AI avatars can run their virtual town without human intervention. These capabilities may offer a glimpse of what some experts think is the beginning of human obsolesce. [15]

REFLECTION: AI AND POLITICS

> *"It seems safe to assume that artificially intelligent systems will not replace humans at the top level of decision-making. But they will be an increasingly significant part of the context in which human decision-makers operate."*
> - Chatham House Report, Q8 UK (Artificial Intelligence and International Affairs)

Personal Note:

PRINCIPLES AND PRACTICES OF HUMANISING ARTIFICIAL INTELLIGENCE

The Consequence of Ethics in Humanising Artificial Intelligence

The relevance and meaning of ethics in humanising AI are fundamental to making AI applications human-friendly, trustworthy, fair, transparent, and accountable. Understanding and managing human-machine relationships in this age and beyond requires a deep understanding of the dynamics of ethics and decision-making relative to human beliefs, cultures, and socio-economic factors as they influence and affect various domains and disciplines such as business, government, education, leadership, media and journalism, health, hospitality, innovation, and technology etc.

The meaning and theories of ethics in decision-making are represented by the viewpoints from which individuals, organisations and communities operate. The theories discussed in this book emphasise different viewpoints, decision-making styles, and rules as they determine the outcome as society and individuals follow their duties to others and fulfil ethically correct decisions. To understand ethics in personal and professional fields, it is important to highlight a standard set of goals or principles that decision-makers seek to achieve to be successful. As explained below, four goals include beneficence, least harm, respect for autonomy, and justice.[1]

Ethical Principle	Description
Beneficence	The principle of beneficence guides the decision-maker to do what is right and good. This priority to "do good" makes an ethical perspective and solution to an ethical dilemma acceptable. This principle is also related to the principle of utility, which states that we should attempt to generate the largest ratio of good over evil possible in the world. The goal of ethical theories is to achieve the best for the benefit of people, according to this principle. This principle is mainly associated with the utilitarian ethical theory discussed in the next section.
Least Harm	Similar to beneficence, least harm deals with situations in which no choice appears beneficial. In such cases, decision-makers seek to choose to do the least harm possible and to do harm to the fewest people. People might argue that a position taken, or a viewpoint, has a greater responsibility to "do no harm" than to benefit others. For example, a customer is more responsible for not buying a product or service from a manufacturer that is faulty or substandard rather than making derogatory remarks about the product and the manufacturer even though the customer had not bought the product.
Respect for Autonomy	This principle states that decision-making should focus on allowing people to be autonomous—to make decisions that apply to their lives. Thus, people should have control over their lives as much as possible because they are the only people who entirely understand their chosen lifestyle. The question is, are there limits to autonomy? Everyone deserves respect because only he/she has had those exact life experiences and intimately understands his emotions, motivations, and physical capabilities. This

Ethical Principle	Description
	ethical principle extends the ethical principle of beneficence because an independent person usually prefers control over his life experiences to obtain the lifestyle that he enjoys.
Justice	The justice ethical principle states that decision-makers should focus on actions that are fair to those involved. This means that ethical decisions should be consistent with the ethical theory unless extenuating circumstances that can be justified exist in the case. This also means that cases with extenuating circumstances must contain a significant and vital difference from similar cases that justifies the inconsistent decision.

The Theories of Ethics in Humanising Innovations

Technology innovations, to be trustworthy with humane qualities, must deal with an ethical dilemma which enforces the need for the design, development and use of AI applications and technology solutions that are deemed ethically acceptable according to principles, guidelines, regulations, and laws which are broadly based on four major categories of ethical theories which include deontology, utilitarianism, common good, and virtues as discussed and characterised below. [2]

1. Deontology (Kantianism Ethics)

This ethical lens focuses on moral rules, rights, principles, and duties. It requires careful ethical reflection and judgment. The ethical issues and concerns include Autonomy (the extent to which people can freely choose for themselves), Dignity (the extent to which people are valued in themselves, not as objects with a price) and Transparency (honest, open, and informed conditions of social treatment/distribution)

Major Deontology Ethics Questions for Technologists and Innovations

- What rights of others and duties to others must we respect in a particular context?
- How might this project impact the dignity and autonomy of each stakeholder?
- Does our project treat people in ways that are transparent and to which they would consent?
- Are our choices/conduct of the sort that I/we could find universally acceptable?
- Does this project involve any conflicting moral duties to others or conflicting stakeholder rights? If so, how can we prioritise these?
- Which moral rights/duties in this project may be justifiably overridden by higher ethical duties or more fundamental rights?

Example of Deontological Ethical Issues in Technology Practice

In what way does a virtual banking assistant deliberately designed to deceive users (for example, by actively representing itself as a human) violate a moral rule or principle, such as the Kantian imperative to never treat a person as a mere means to an end?

Would people be justified in feeling wronged by the bank upon discovering the deceit, even if the software had not financially harmed them?

Does a participant in a commercial or financial transaction have a moral right not to be lied to, even if a legal loophole means no legal right is violated here?

2. Utilitarian Ethics

Characteristics of Utilitarian Ethics

It is a common practice among many engineers to adopt this theory, as it implies the ability to quantify the ethical analysis and select the optimal outcome while equally considering the welfare of all affected stakeholders.

The ethical issues and concerns frequently highlighted by looking through this ethical lens include, but are not limited to, happiness (in a comprehensive sense, including such factors as physical, mental, and other forms of well-being); balancing of stakeholder interests (who is benefitting and who is being harmed, in what ways and to what degree, and how many); and prediction of consequences (some consequences can be predicted and others cannot; still, one should account for all reasonably foreseeable effects of this action).

Major Utilitarian Ethics Questions for Technologists and Innovations

- Who are all the people likely to be directly and indirectly affected by this project? In what ways?
- Will the effects in aggregate likely create more good than harm, and what types of good and harm? What are we counting as well-being, and what are we counting as harm/suffering?
- What are this project's most morally significant harms and benefits? Is our view of these concepts too narrow, or are we thinking about all relevant types of harm/benefit (psychological, political, environmental, moral, cognitive, emotional, institutional, cultural)
- How might future generations be affected by this project?
- Have we adequately considered 'dual use' and downstream effects other than those we intend?
- Have we considered the full range of actions/resources/opportunities available to us that might?
- Can boosting this project's potential benefits and minimising its risks?
- Are we settling too quickly for an ethically 'acceptable' design or goal ('do no harm'), or are there missed opportunities to set a higher ethical standard and generate even greater benefits?

Characteristics of Utilitarian Ethics

Example of Problems with Utilitarian Ethics in Technology Practice

However, there are some problems with utilitarian ethics such as comparing and measuring the consequences of alternative actions is very difficult as there will be a tendency to ignore the consequences, especially the harmful consequences, to anyone other than those closest to us and the question of whether the ends justify the means whereby it is not clear if there are certain decisions that should follow no matter what the consequences?

3. Common Good Perspective of Ethics

Characteristics of Common Good Perspective of Ethics

The common good perspective of ethics focuses on the impact of a practice on the health and welfare of communities or groups of people. The focus is on groups such as:

- Communities (of varying scales, ranging from families to neighbourhoods, towns, provinces, nations, and the world)
- Relationships (not only among individuals but also relationships in a more holistic sense of groups, including nonhuman animals and the natural world as well)
- Institutions of governance (and how these networked institutions interact with each other)
- Economic institutions (including corporations and corporate cultures, trade organisations, etc.)
- Other social institutions (such as religious groups, alum associations, professional associations, environmental groups, etc.)

Major Questions About Common Good Ethics for Technologists and Innovations

- Does this project benefit many individuals, but only at the expense of the common good?
- Does it do the opposite by sacrificing individuals' welfare or critical interests for the common good? Have we considered these trade-offs and determined which are ethically justifiable?

Characteristics of Common Good Perspective of Ethics

- What might this technology do for or to social institutions such as various levels of government, schools, hospitals, churches, infrastructure, and so on?
- What might this technology do for or to the larger environment beyond human society, such as ecosystems, biodiversity, sustainability, climate change, animal welfare, etc.?

4. Virtue (Character-Based) Ethics

Characteristics of Virtue (Character-Based) Ethics

Virtue ethics is concerned with the rightness or wrongness of individual actions. A right act is the action a virtuous person would do in the same circumstances. This type of ethics theory also guides the sort of characteristics and behaviours a reasonable person will seek to achieve.

However, in cultural terms, there is no general agreement on what virtues are.

Central Question About Virtue (Character-Based) Ethics for Technologists and Innovations

- What design habits are we regularly embodying, and are they the habits of excellent designers?
- Would we want future generations of technologists to use our practice as an example to follow?
- What habits of character will this design/project foster in users and other affected stakeholders?
- Will this design/project weaken or disincentivise any important human habits, skills, or virtues that are central to human excellence (moral, political, or intellectual)? Will it strengthen any?
- Will this design/project incentivise any vicious habits or traits in users or other stakeholders?
- Do our choices and practices embody the appropriate 'mean' of conduct (relative to the context)? Or are they extreme (excessive or deficient) in some ways?
- Is there anything unusual about the context of this project that requires us to reconsider or modify the regular 'script' of good design practice? Are we qualified and able to safely

and ethically modify normal design practice, and if not, who is?

- What will this design/project say about us as people in the eyes of those who receive it?
- Will we, as individuals and as a team/organisation, be proud to have our names associated with this project one day?

Ethics and Governance of Humanising Artificial Intelligence

It is well known that new technology brings new challenges, including ethical issues and dilemmas. The salient question exists of how new technologies or innovations should be regulated and managed as they can be employed and deployed for illegal or harmful activities even though the same can be used for the benefit of society. Aside from the unknown harms and risks associated with AI applications, concerted efforts are being channelled to eliminate, mitigate, and manage the known potential harms due to bias, discrimination, misinformation and disinformation, invasion of privacy, etc.

Exploring the meaning of AI ethics in humanising artificial intelligence involves applying a set of values, principles, and techniques that employ widely accepted standards to guide moral conduct in the development and use of AI systems.[3] The ethics of artificial intelligence is a branch of the ethics of technology specific to artificially intelligent applications vis-a-vis ethical and moral values in the interactions of humans with AI's lifecycle, which includes conceptualisation, design, development, deployment, use and decommissioning of the AI system.

The Global Perspective of Ethics for Technology and Artificial Intelligence

The global perspective of ethics enjoins that technologists remain vigilant and humble enough to remember that whatever ethical frameworks may be most familiar or 'natural' to them and their colleagues, they only amount to a tiny fraction of the ways of seeing the ethical landscape that their potential users and affected communities may adopt.

Technologists should design, develop, and deploy with ethical values in mind and do so in ways that are careful, reflective, explicit, humble, transparent, and responsive to stakeholder feedback and not in ways that are arrogant, opaque, and irresponsible. To further address this, the following questions are pertinent as guides to the design, development, and use of technology and AI applications from global perspectives:

- Have we invited and considered the ethical perspectives of users and communities other than ours, including those quite culturally or physically remote from us? Or have we fallen into the trap of "designing for ourselves"?

- How might the impacts and perceptions of this design/project differ for users and communities with very different value systems and social norms than those local or familiar to us? If we don't know, how can we learn the answer?

- The vision of the 'good life' dominant in tech-centric cultures of the West is far from universal. Have we considered the global reach of technology and that ethical traditions beyond the West often emphasise values such as social harmony and care, hierarchical respect, honour, personal sacrifice, or social ritual far more than we might?

- In what cases should we refuse, for compelling ethical reasons, to honour the social norms of another tradition, and in what cases should we incorporate and uphold others' norms?

- How will we decide, and by what standard or process?

Taming the Algorithm - Seeking the Balanced Trade-offs

Widely reported in the media recently is a news headline: *"European companies claim the EU's AI Act* could *'jeopardise Europe's competitiveness and technological sovereignty"*. The AI Act is a proposed European law on artificial intelligence (AI), and it would be the first law on AI by a major regulator anywhere. Over 150 executives from companies like Renault, Heineken, Airbus, and Siemens signed the letter asking the EU to reconsider their AI regulation plans. *(The ongoing updates on the EU's AI Act are available here [4i & 4ii])*

On June 2023, the European Parliament green-lit a draft of the AI Act, which is over two years in the making, developing its rules and expanding them to encompass recent AI breakthroughs like large language AI models (LLMs) and foundation models, such as OpenAI's GPT-4. The signatories of the open letter claim that the AI Act in its current state may suppress the opportunity AI technology provides for Europe to *"re-join the technological avant-garde."* They argue that the approved rules are too extreme and risk undermining the bloc's technological ambitions instead of providing a suitable environment for AI innovation.[5]

Guidelines, Principles, Frameworks, Methodologies and Toolkits

Guidelines, principles, frameworks, methodologies, toolkits, and practices are to guide and assist all stakeholders in the process of design, development, deployment, and decommissioning. These provide tested and tried ways, advice, and recommendations of how to manage the lifecycle of AI applications, even where there is no laid-out policy and standard. All these guidelines, principles, practices, frameworks, methodologies, and toolkits raise awareness of the potential impact of AI on society, the environment, consumers, workers, and citizens (children and people belonging to marginalised groups). They encourage the involvement of all relevant stakeholders in the co-creation, co-production, and oversight processes of the applications.

In the design, development and use of any AI application, there are core areas or requirements, according to the proposed EU Act, that are primary requirements before an AI application can be adjudged to be responsible, sustainable, and trustworthy in society. The core areas are:

Fundamental Rights and Algorithm Impact Assessment (FRAIA)

Fundamental rights encompass rights such as human dignity and non-discrimination, as well as rights about data protection and privacy, to name just some examples. Before self-assessing an AI system with this Assessment List, a fundamental rights and algorithm impact assessment (FRAIA[6]) should be performed. This fundamental rights and algorithm impact assessment (FRAIA) is a discussion and decision-making tool for government and non-government organisations. The tool facilitates an interdisciplinary dialogue by those responsible for the development and use of an algorithmic system such as AI.

The commissioning client is primarily responsible for the (delegated) implementation of the FRAIA as tools and metrics designed to help AI actors develop and use trustworthy AI systems and applications that respect human rights and are fair, transparent, explainable, robust, secure, and safe. A FRAIA could include questions such as the following: [6.]

Ref	Rights	Description	Oversight Practice	Mitigation or Redress Practice
1	Human Right	Can the AI system discriminate against people based on sex, race, colour, religion, disability, age, or sexual orientation?	Are there any procedures in place to detect and prevent bias in the AI system during its development, launch, and usage?	Have you implemented processes to address and rectify potential harmful discrimination (bias) in the AI system?
2	Children's Right	Does the AI system respect the child's rights, for example, regarding child Protection and considering the child's best interests?	Have you implemented processes to address and rectify potential harm to children by the AI system?	Have you put in place processes to test and monitor for potential harm to children during the development, deployment, and use phases of the AI system?
3	Personal Data	Does the AI system protect personal data relating to individuals in line with GDPR?	Have you put in place processes to assess the need for a data protection impact assessment, including evaluating the necessity and proportionality of the processing operations about their purpose regarding the development, deployment, and use phases of the AI system?	Are there measures envisaged in place to address the risks, including safeguards, security measures, and mechanisms, to ensure the protection of personal data regarding the development, deployment, and use phases of the AI system?
4	Freedom of Expression	Does the AI system respect freedom of expression, information, and	Have you put in place processes to test and monitor for potential	Have you established methods to address freedom of expression

Ref	Rights	Description	Oversight Practice	Mitigation or Redress Practice
		freedom of assembly and association?	infringement on freedom of expression and information and freedom of assembly and association during the development, deployment, and use phases of the AI system?	and assembly infringements in the AI system?

Table 2.1: Sample of Fundamental Rights and Algorithm Impact Assessment (FRAIA) List

The Ethics Guidelines for Trustworthy AI

In ethical management of the lifecycle of AI applications, it is crucial to pay close attention to processes and procedures underpinning their design, development, and use. The ongoing effort by the High-Level Expert Group on Artificial Intelligence (AI HLEG), as established by the European Commission in 2018, provides AI ethical guidelines that highlight seven essential requirements that AI-based applications need to meet to be trustworthy and ethically sound.[7]

It is important to note that these requirements apply to all stakeholders, including developers, deployers and end-users. Each stakeholder has a specific role to ensure that it adheres to these requirements.[8] As shown in the figure below, it should be noted that the interrelationship and interdependence of the seven requirements and their ethics attributes are of the same importance as they support each other, and this interrelationship should be continuously evaluated and addressed throughout the lifecycle of all AI applications and data management.

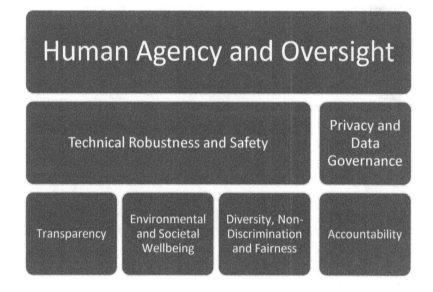

Figure 2.1: The Seven Requirements of Ethics Guideline[8]

According to The Ethics Guidelines[8] for Trustworthy Artificial Intelligence (AI), these seven requirements are defined below:

1. **Human Agency and Oversight:** This requirement helps to ensure that AI applications do not challenge and weaken human rights and autonomy or cause other harm to humans. It requires AI-based systems to support human autonomy and decision-making. Oversight may be achieved through governance

mechanisms such as a human-in-the-loop (HITL), human-on-the-loop (HOTL), or human-in-command (HIC) approach. HITL refers to the capability for human intervention in every decision cycle of the system, which is neither possible nor desirable at various times. HOTL refers to the capability for human intervention during the system's design cycle and monitoring of the system's operation. HIC refers to the capability to oversee the overall activity of the AI system (including its broader economic, societal, legal, and ethical impact) and the ability to decide when and how to use the system in any situation.

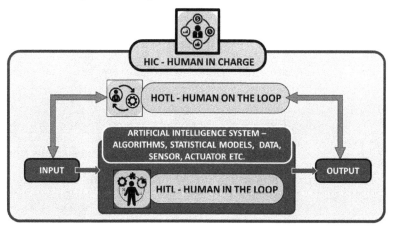

Figure 2.2: Trustworthy AI Requirements for Human Agency and Oversight

2. **Technical Robustness and Safety:** A crucial component of achieving trustworthy AI is technical

robustness, which is closely linked to the principle of prevention of harm. Technical robustness requires that AI systems be developed with a preventative approach to risks and in a manner such that they reliably behave as intended while minimising unintentional and unexpected harm and preventing unacceptable harm. This should also apply to potential changes in their operating environment or the presence of other agents (human and artificial) that may interact with the system in an adversarial manner. In addition, we should ensure the physical and mental integrity of humans.

3. **Privacy and Data Governance**: Closely linked to the principle of prevention of harm is privacy, a fundamental right affected by AI systems. Prevention of harm to privacy also causes adequate data governance that covers the quality and integrity of the data used, its relevance considering the domain in which the AI systems will be deployed, its access protocols and the capability to process data in a manner that protects privacy.

4. **Transparency:** The developed systems should have traceability and explainability functions as required. The datasets, procedures, and algorithms used

should be documented to allow traceability and to explain all the processes involved in the automated decision produced.

5. **Diversity, Non-Discrimination, and Fairness:** The practice of equality, inclusion and diversity should be considered when developing an AI-based system. We must prevent unfairness and bias and make the system accessible and accountable for everyone's culture and values.

6. **Environmental and Societal Wellbeing:** The AI-based systems should be useful to everyone as a human being and contribute to the development of a responsible society and sustainable environment by directly tackling essential issues such as climate change, resource degradation, energy consumption, crime investigation, etc.

7. **Accountability:** The requirement of accountability involves the implementation of processes to ensure responsibility and accountability of the AI-based systems and their output. This should be done before and after the development, deployment, and use of the AI system or service. Also, when an unjust adverse impact occurs, accessible mechanisms

should be foreseen to ensure adequate redress. Public trust is gained when it is known that such redress mechanisms are in place.

Data Ethics Frameworks of Trustworthy AI Applications

The data ethics framework is a set of principles and procedures put in place to regulate the use of data within an organisation. The UK government first published the UK Data Ethics Framework in 2018, and this was later amended in 2020. We split the structure of the UK data framework into different principles and actions that need to be considered in the AI-based system's lifecycle. This process has been given a score between zero and five, where zero is an unacceptable outcome, and five is the outcome that meets all the principles.[9]

Figure 3 below outlines five specific actions and three principles necessary for a data ethics framework. The principles include transparency, accountability, and fairness. The actions include defining public benefit/user needs, involving diverse expertise, complying with the law, reviewing data quality/limitations, and evaluating broader policy implications. The combination of these three principles and five actions is necessary to ensure that the system complies with the ethics and regulations of the sector.[9]

Overarching Principles	Description	Specific Actions
Transparency	This principle states that the organisation building an AI-based system needs to make all actions, procedures, and data open to inspection and publish them in a format that is accessible to everyone. It underscores how much information, methods, and outcomes about AI applications and data management are publicly available.	1. **Define and Understand the Public Benefit and Need:** When starting any new project in AI and Data, the purpose must be defined, and the target customers must be identified. Apart from that, all the goals must be clear and achievable, and the needs of the end-users must be clearly stated as well 2. **Involve Diverse Expertise:** Create a team or multiple teams with diverse expertise; this helps to bring a multidisciplinary, extensive range of skills and experiences.
Accountability	The second principle is accountability and how the book must incorporate an effective governance and oversight process. This is important to ensure that the objectives assigned are met and that they respond to the general needs of society. It underscores the established mechanisms and extents of public	3. **Comply with the Law:** When building AI-based applications, you need to be familiar with all the regulations and laws related to Artificial Intelligence and Data. 4. **Review the Quality and Limitations of the Data:** The organisation

Overarching Principles	Description	Specific Actions
	scrutiny, governance and peer review of the design, development and use of AI applications and data management.	implementing the AI-based system or service needs to ensure that the data are accurate, representative and in good quality.
Fairness	The last principle is fairness; this helps to remove any form of discrimination in the system's life cycle, engendering togetherness and belongingness. It underscores the extent of the alignment of the design, development and use of AI applications and data management without discrimination, harm, or detriment to any group in society. It promotes just and fair outcomes for all.	5. **Evaluation and Consider Wider Policy Implications:** The process must be regularly evaluated to ensure that the outcomes are correctly used and to consider the broad implications of the process. The evaluation plan needs to be efficient and robust.

Table 2.2: Framework of Data Ethics and Requirements

Legislation and Regulatory Frameworks of Trustworthy AI

As earlier highlighted, in an open letter, more than 150 top executives from European businesses have openly criticised the EU AI Act. They argue that the proposed regulations risk undermining European competitiveness and technological self-reliance. The group has also highlighted concerns about overly stringent rules, particularly for generative AI systems, and the potential for disproportionate compliance costs and liability risks.

All technologies, including artificial Intelligence applications and solutions alike, have weaknesses, limitations, and undesired effects. These limitations lead to some legislative and regulatory complications, as the use of AI-based systems for any purpose has inherent risks and undermines fundamental human rights, privacy, democracy, civil liberties, etc.

The European Union has implemented different legal frameworks to facilitate legislation and regulation of AI applications. The GDPR (General Data Protection Regulation), being an EU's effort in this direction, is a set of principles, procedures and legal regulations aimed at providing efficient legal precautions for stakeholders and players alike (Designers, Deployers, Suppliers, Users, Policy Makers, etc.) as they include user's rights of transparency, explanation, getting human intervention and contestation of the decisions coming out from the AI-based system in the processing of user's data, etc.[10]

However, other nations and global bodies are developing legislative and regulatory principles, guidelines, frameworks, and toolkits, as explained below, to facilitate the design, development, deployment, and use of trustworthy AI solutions in society. To overcome the problems, global bodies are encouraging and recommending manufacturers and suppliers of AI-based systems to implement and consider all the requirements necessary to support human review from the early phase of design, provide appropriate training for human reviewers and provide skills and tools required to address users' concerns, and if required override automated decisions. [10]

Ethical Toolkit as Case Study: Alethia by Rolls-Royce – A Practical and Industry-Based Toolkit

Based on global and industry relevance, the toolkit developed by Rolls-Royce called 'The Aletheia' for building and supporting trustworthy AI has been selected as a case study. The Aletheia Framework™ [11] is a toolkit for ethics and trustworthiness in artificial intelligence believed to be useful in helping any organisation navigate the day-to-day intricacies of applying AI that can build public trust in the technology.

Artificial intelligence ethics is a complex area, and a tool like The Aletheia Framework can help reassure organisations, people, and communities that the ethical implications of an AI have been fully considered; it is as fair as possible in making trustworthy decisions. In-depth and practical analyses of Aletheia

Framework, which is built on Rolls-Royce's decades of over 70 trillion data points across 26 dimensions on jet engines and other products, is to help in improved efficiency and sustainability, safety, and deep ethical culture, thereby fulfilling the potential of artificial intelligence to support the health, wealth and growth of society which can only be realised with public trust.

The Aletheia Framework is a practical one-page toolkit guide for developers, executives, and boards both before deploying an AI and during its use. It asks them to consider 32 facets of social impact, governance, trust and transparency and to provide evidence that can then engage with approvers, stakeholders, or auditors. A new module added in December 2021 is a tried and tested way to identify and help mitigate the risk of bias in training data and AIs. This complements the existing five-step continuous automated checking process, which, if comprehensively applied, tracks the decisions the AI makes to detect bias in service or malfunction and allow human intervention to control and correct it.

To keep up with changes in the global landscape of trustworthy AI, Roll Royce is collaborating with many sectors – including music, oncology, and education – and receiving brilliant feedback. It is also taking inputs on AI ethics from global bodies, including UNESCO's recent recommendations, and this has encouraged the publication of The Aletheia Framework v2.0, which is simpler and more relevant to a broader range of sectors, as well as a much wider range of organisations, from start-ups to large corporations.

Major Toolkits and Resources for Humanising AI and Data Management

As shown later in Chapter 9 is the glossary of frameworks, tool kits, principles, oaths, manifestoes, codes of conduct, policy papers, white papers, statements, reports, and other resources of ethics and governance of humanising AI and Data management. The list is not exhaustive, as the global landscapes of AI innovations and humanisation are dynamic and ever-evolving.

REFLECTION: AI AND ETHICS

> *"I'm increasingly inclined to think that there should be some regulatory oversight, maybe at the national and international level, just to make sure that we don't do something very foolish. I mean with artificial intelligence we're summoning the demon."*
> - Elon Musk[Q4] (A Businessman and Investor, CEO/(Founder) of SpaceX, Angel Investor, Tesla, X Corp, xAI, Neuralink, OpenAI among others)

Personal Note:

RISKS AND THREATS IN HUMAN-MACHINE COLLABORATIONS

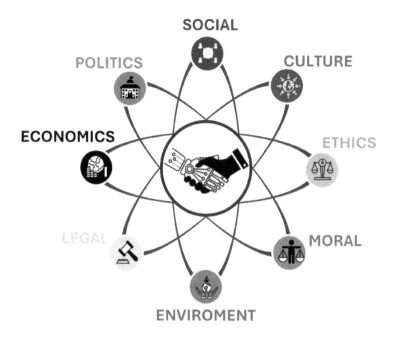

Figure 3.1: Human-Machine Sociotechnical Interaction Framework

Sociotechnical Dimensions of Human-Machine Interaction and Collaborations

The pertinent question being asked by the vast majority of stakeholders is: when and to what extent do we trust machines to make crucial, life-or-death decisions? Exploring the inherent risks, threats, and issues of AI applications in society, AI robots at a news conference with a panel of AI-enabled humanoid social robots at a global summit in Geneva, Switzerland, reckon they could run the world better. But with this comes the caveat that humans should proceed with caution when adopting and embracing the exponential growth in AI and its applications.

They joined around 3,000 experts in the field to harness the power of AI — and channel it into being used to solve some of the world's most pressing problems, such as climate change, hunger, and social care.[1]

The new frontiers that are opening to humanity owing to aggressive technology advancements require multi-cultural, forward-looking, adaptable, and integrated measures which include a risk-based approach to mitigating and managing the threats and issues in the entire lifecycle of design, development, deployment, and decommissioning of AI applications. These concerted proactive efforts should compel and constrain all players and stakeholders (developers, deployers, users, countries, competent authorities, etc.) to proactively identify, define, assess, and understand associated potential threats and risks involved in their domains and works and aggressively take appropriate mitigation and control measures in addressing the risks in fulfilling their respective obligation and responsibility.

Rooting out bias in AI applications requires a focus on addressing systemic and human biases. The analyses in this book, therefore, take a deeper look at all the AI-associated sociotechnical risk factors in technology design, deployment and use with their varying probability of occurrence and severity as related to all human domains (social, political, economic, environmental, moral, ethical, cultural, and legal) as further highlighted in Figure 3.1.

Categories of AI Applications and Risk Level

The momentum of the penetration and adoption of AI-based solutions by individuals and society has grown exponentially in recent years. Therefore, there is an urgent and pertinent need to implement robust oversight and regulations on its use in society in ethical, lawful, and robust ways in societal service. The analyses of the global ramifications of the risks and issues relating to AI solutions concerning social, political, economic, environmental, moral, ethical, cultural, and legal domains, and how to use a collaborative and interactive tool (solution) to standardise the trustworthiness of their use are the main thrusts of this publication.

The EU's Regulatory Framework on AI (The Artificial Intelligence Act[2]) which assesses the risk of AI-based products, services, systems, and practices, categorises AI-based risks into four levels of severity and impact as listed below:

RISK LEVEL	DESCRIPTION	FEATURE & FUNCTION
Unacceptable Risk	AI systems considered a clear threat to people's safety, livelihoods, and rights will be banned or prohibited. It also includes AI applications with unjustifiable, inadmissible, and serious potential for harm.	Social scoring, facial recognition and mass surveillance, behavioural manipulation, etc.
High Risk	AI systems identified as high risk are subject to a deep risk assessment, conformity	Access to education, employment,

RISK LEVEL	DESCRIPTION	FEATURE & FUNCTION
	assessment, mitigation strategy, high-quality datasets, traceability, documentation, clear explainability protocols to the user, and a high level of robustness, security, and accuracy. It also includes AI applications with significant potential for harm.	justice, immigration, law, public services, safety component of vehicles, etc.
Limited Risk	This level of risk imposes machine transparency as a requirement and obligation. It also includes AI applications with some potential for harm.	Chatbots, deep fakes, emotion recognition, biometric categorisation, impersonation, etc.
Minimal Risk	This level of risk requires no obligation but voluntary compliance or code of conduct to any of the regulatory requirements. It also includes AI applications with negligible or zero potential for harm.	Video games, spam filters, etc.

Table 3.2: Category of Risk and AI Application

Multi-dimensional Analyses of Risk in AI Applications

The human-machine interactions in various aspects of life have proven to be laden with inherent risks and constraints. These encompass social, political, economic, environmental, moral, ethical, cultural, and legal interactions and issues. To this end, these issues need to be reflectively ingrained in the design, deployment and use of AI-based products, services, and applications (solutions). The inherent and potential risks and challenges majorly exist in the areas of errors because of deviation from ethical standards, system limitations, and intentional and unintentional biases, which have huge ramifications on society and the reputation of the government and non-government organisations involved.

Social Risk Factor

Research findings largely support that AI-based technologies, e.g., facial recognition software, may incorporate intentional and unintentional racial and gender biases. Studies by the *Civil Liberties Union* and *MIT 2022* found that Amazon's *Rekognition* technology misidentifies women and people of colour more frequently than it does white men.[3] This social risk and other relevant ones, with their high rate of probability of occurrence and varying degrees of severity, are expected to be assessed or evaluated to mitigate or remove their potential impacts on individuals and society.

Moral Risk (hazard) Factor

A moral risk in the design, deployment and use of AI applications is when an individual or an organisation intentionally introduces or exposes itself to harmful, insecure, and unsafe practices and processes for financial gain knowing fully well that the risk and fallout is to be borne by a third party.

According to a paper published by Stanford University, CA, on this kind of risk, most technology manufacturers face this moral hazard where they must decide whether to make (or later fail to support) devices having risks that would be costly or impossible to eliminate for users - when those users will probably pay the same to them regardless.[4]

Environmental Risk Factor

Using technology constitutes an environmental risk with a massive threat to climate change and sustainable living. Regardless of the ecological risk impact on the development and operation of AI applications, an assessment of the effects of this risk factor is also germane to a sustainable planet. Every element of AI-based solution or technology requires energy consumption with a carbon cost and massive carbon footprint of carbon emission through inefficient energy or electricity consumption, e.g., training and developing one machine neural architecture costs about 626,000 tons of CO_2 emission.[5]

Ethical Risk Factor

The primary purpose of ethical risk assessment of the design, deployment and use of AI solutions is to ultimately achieve and justify public trustworthiness by balancing the requirements of privacy and civil liberties with security and safety. Allied to this is mitigating and removing the potential negative impact of the occurrence of such risk on individual and society. The ethical risk analyses considered in a later section of risk assessment and management are based on the arguments from proponents and opponents of AI-based solutions in society. And if the risks, problems, and challenges outweigh the value and benefits of deploying the system in society. These ethical risk factors are mainly related to racial bias, erosion of civil liberties, gender discrimination, ambiguous success and acceptance metrics, limitations in explainability, transparency, accountability, public oversight, etc.

Legal Risk Factor

Legal risk exists in the design and deployment of technology, implying that palpable legal consequences may subsist with possible penalties for actions emanating from non-compliance with legal requirements in technology, which may lead to financial or reputational loss.[6] An excellent example of court actions due to lack of proper risk assessment and management is the case in August 2020, where the Court of Appeal of England and Wales found that the use of facial recognition technology by South Wales Police had been unlawful due to how the system was deployed and the discovered gender and racial biases.[7]

Economic Risk Factor

Profit over people. The growing digital capitalism that seeks to monetise digital technologies and AI solutions solely focuses on sales and market size rather than on social good is a considerable risk and concern. AI technologies or applications are transforming global productivity and GDP (Gross Domestic Production) with a projected contribution of $ 15.7 trillion to the global economy. There is also a 26% boost to global GDP and approximately 300 new use cases by 2030.[8] However, the potential risks of the solutions being driven majorly for commercial gains at the expense of human needs are also enormous. These call for an urgent, robust, and all-encompassing risk assessment and management agenda on a global scale.

Political Risk Factor

With the evolution of artificial intelligence in the last decade, particularly with the development of machine-learning algorithms, there has been significant progress in the many use cases of these technologies. However, with these advancements comes the potential political risk factor that affects privacy and civil liberties. According to a leading scientific paper published by *Scientific Report* and backed by *Stanford University,*[9] on 25 November 2021, ubiquitous facial recognition technology can expose individuals' political orientation, as the faces of liberals and conservatives consistently differ.

A facial recognition algorithm was applied to naturalistic images of 1,085,795 individuals to predict their political orientation by comparing their similarity to the faces of liberals, conservatives, and others. Political orientation was correctly classified in 72%

of liberal–conservative face pairs. Accuracy was similar across countries (the U.S., Canada, and the UK), environments (Facebook and dating websites), and when faces were compared across samples. Accuracy remained high (69%) even when controlling for age, gender, and ethnicity. Given the widespread use of facial recognition, these findings have critical implications for protecting privacy and civil liberties.[9]

Cultural Risk Factor

The recent national surveys of the data on values and beliefs of people in the countries that are members of the World Values Survey Association (WVSA) reveal the cultural beliefs of the public in different and diverse cultures as in different countries under investigation.[10] The public perception and acceptance of AI-based solutions, especially facial recognition technology by law enforcement agencies, are in various cultures. Based on this online survey conducted among the internet-connected population in China, Germany, the United Kingdom, and the United States, the study finds that facial recognition technology enjoys the highest acceptance among general respondents in China. In contrast, acceptance is lowest in Germany, and the United Kingdom and the United States are in between.[11]

Existing and Emerging Trust Issues in Human-Machine Relationship

In the conceptualisation, design, development, deployment, use and maintenance of AI solutions, consequent trust (ethical) issues have generated concerns. These have also highlighted the need to incorporate robust mechanisms into the frameworks, legislation and regulations binding on all stakeholders in the field. The following section highlights these critical trust and ethical issues. It discusses some available guidelines, principles, processes, standards, frameworks, legislation, regulations, and the global best practices in place to resolve, mitigate and manage these ethical issues.

Although Artificial Intelligence has brought many advantages to daily lives and business operations, the design and use of AI have led to severe ethical issues that have negatively impacted human rights, safety, security, well-being, dignity, and autonomy. In the recent past, academics and some not-for-profit organisations were concerned about these ethics and data governance issues of AI. But presently, most businesses, especially the big corporations and global organisations, are investing in mechanisms to tackle and address ethical problems that result from the use of massive data and AI algorithms.[12]

Data governance and ethical policy are tailored to a specific business or area; however, some critical ethical issues are common to all applications, services and products that involve Artificial intelligence. As follows:

- *Opportunity Loss*: AI-driven applications, products, and services come with the system or machine making biased choices and decisions due to how the algorithm or model has been trained, intentionally or unintentionally, on the available datasets. This can lead to job or opportunity loss for people of a certain demography.[13]

- *Bias in Data*: Intentional and unintentional biases in these algorithms and data selection can be damaging for victims. AI applications are highly vulnerable to biases, and various errors are usually introduced through a disproportionate dataset for training and testing the machine learning models.

- *Overly-Dependency on AI and AI Autonomy*: As society is becoming more dependent on AI applications and technologies in decision-making, recruitment, product development, etc., the major concerns are the potential risk and severe impact they may have if these AI technologies are compromised, suffer a breakdown and out of control and supervision therefore operating independent of direct human intervention, but within constraints, to achieve a goal or solve a problem.

- *Deepfakes*: One major ethical issue that has significant ramifications for society is the AI application in Deepfakes, which occurs when an AI machine learning model is used to fake or camouflage the audio and video of humans in video presentations or movies. A recent example is the December 2020 Channel 4's deepfake Queen's Speech (which sparked nearly 400 Ofcom complaints). Deepfakes pose unique reputational risks and potential infringement of personality rights. Whereas a written false statement may not be accepted as truth by the reader, material purporting to make up real video evidence is unlikely to be questioned similarly.[14]

- *Lack of Trust*: The public trust in using AI, especially in decision-making, is still very low as there are many reasons, but the most common reason is related to the system's bias and lack of clarity and education on most of the automated decisions that are made by the AI systems.[15]

- *Loss of Human Insight and Intervention*: The use of AI can help augment outcomes and important decisions, whilst the lack of human intervention in the process can lead to a loss of some valuable insights, thereby introducing unintended and intended biases.[16]

- *Ambiguous Standards of Success or Success Metrics*: This raises a fundamental question when evaluating an AI's accuracy, transparency, or fairness. What is the relevant standard of success? As well noted, human decision-makers are far from perfect for being influenced by racial bias, and a familiar chorus among critics of predictive technologies is that predictive systems will discriminate against people of colour. There is a need to detect what constitutes adequate and acceptable performance by data-driven systems such that any organisation or agency is justified in implementing and operating it in their decision-making process.[17]

- *Limited or Lack of Explainability and Transparency:* The opacity of the design and implementation of predictive AI, like many other algorithmic systems, has been criticised for its relative lack of transparency and regarded as a "black box". A system is opaque and non-transparent when the input of a feature or some features cannot be understood or explained in the light of the output or the final prediction by the human designer, the decision-maker, and the affected person.[17]

- *Lack of Accountability and Community oversight:* The appropriate mechanisms for holding the manufacturers accountable as a public institution are very important in this dispensation. The establishment and use of these accountability mechanisms foster public trust, enable the achievement of valuable institutional goals, and identify and address any problematic elements within the institution itself. But the value of accountability is also an intrinsic part of what constitutes a legitimate institution, particularly those, like law enforcement, that wield significant authority.[17]

- ***Ambiguous Licensing and Liability:*** Organisations involved in developing, licensing or using AI services and products should ensure that their contracts specifically reflect the key risks relating to AI products. Also, they have been appropriately developed and tested, are free of bias, and their use does not infringe on third-party IP (Intellectual Property). Equally, the licensor will want to ensure that the licensee remains liable for any unlawful use of the AI products, e.g., any GDPR breaches.

- **Misinformation:** This is incorrect or false, misleading or inaccurate information that is unintentionally or unknowingly presented in the design, development, and use of AI applications. The definitions of misinformation may differ in cultural contexts as it affects society. Even when retracted, it can continue to influence memory, decisions, actions, and viewpoints.

- **Disinformation:** This is false, inaccurate, or misleading information designed, presented, and promoted to intentionally cause public harm in the design, development, and use of AI applications. According to the MIT paper *The Spread of True and False News Online*, it takes true stories about six times as long to reach 1,500 people as it does for false stories to reach the same number of people.[18]

- **Fake News:** This is perpetrated through fake, false, or regularly misleading websites that are shared on social media. It can also be spread through websites that may circulate misleading and potentially unreliable information and through satire/comedy sites, which can offer vital critical commentary on politics and society but have the potential to be shared as actual/literal news.

- **Unregulated Generative AI and Quantum AI (ChatGPT, AutoGPT, XGPT, Quantum AI):** Another example is an AI model called ChatGPT (Chat Generative Pre-Trained Transformer) is a large language model-based chatbot developed by OpenAI and launched on November 30, 2022,[19] that allows users to interact with it by using prompts or by asking questions represented in text and later in audio and visual formats. ChatGPT scours the internet for data and answers with a poem, Python code, or a proposal. The ethical dilemma is that people use ChatGPT to win coding contests or write essays. It raises similar questions to Lensa but with text rather than images.

Moreover, Auto-GPT is an "AI agent" that, given a goal in natural language, will attempt to achieve it by breaking it into sub-tasks and using the internet and other tools in an automatic loop. Unlike interactive systems such as ChatGPT, which require manual commands for every task, Auto-GPT assigns itself new objectives to work on reaching a greater goal without a mandatory need for human input.[20]

It can execute responses to prompts to accomplish a goal task and, in doing so, will create and revise its prompts to recursive instances in response to new information. Generative AI, future interactive XGPT and quantum AI operating without proper human oversight and participation can cause bigger issues of immense proportion compared to AI that depends on human interventions.

REFLECTION: AI AND CULTURE

"You have to talk about 'The Terminator' if you're talking about artificial intelligence. I actually think that that's way off. I don't think that an artificially intelligent system that has superhuman intelligence will be violent. I do think that it will disrupt our culture."
- Gray Scott[Q6] (Futurist, Philosopher, Artist)

Personal Note:

HUMAN-CENTRIC STRATEGY FOR HUMANISING AI APPLICATIONS

Figure 4.1: Humanising Artificial Intelligence and Trustworthiness

Human-In-The-Loop Is Not Enough

"It's dangerous when it works and even more dangerous when it doesn't work," said Robert Williams,[1] while testifying as California legislature (USA) sat to debate several proposals about the use of the technology by the police. In 2020, Williams was arrested for allegedly stealing thousands of dollars of watches. Detroit police (USA) had matched grainy surveillance footage of the crime to Williams' driver's license photo using a facial recognition service.

But Williams was not the robber. At the time of the robbery, he was driving home from work.

Williams' arrest was the first documented case of someone being wrongfully detained based on facial recognition technology, which police departments and government agencies across the US use. This issue reflects an ongoing debate and tension over the use of surveillance systems worldwide. Several studies show that facial recognition systems regularly misidentify Black and brown people, posing a particular threat to communities that police and surveillance systems have disproportionately targeted.[1]

Major AI Applications that could Transform the Way we Live and Work

Most emerging and exponential technologies and solutions have a form of AI capability. These solutions and technologies powered by AI are being integrated into our daily lives by private and public sectors. The major technologies to watch out for are:

> **Facial Recognition**: In June 2020, IBM, Amazon, and Microsoft announced that they were stepping back from facial recognition software development amid concerns that it reinforces racial and gender bias.

> **Deepfake:** The origins of Deepfake, using AI to create falsified photos, videos, or audio files, can be traced to

2017 when pornographic videos spliced with celebrities' faces were posted online.

AI Drug Discovery: In January 2020, researchers launched the world's first human clinical trial of a drug discovered using AI. Intended to treat obsessive-compulsive disorder (OCD), the compound DSP-1181 was identified using an AI drug discovery platform called *Centaur Chemist.*

Reading Non-Verbal Cues: Emotion AI describes systems that recognise, respond to and simulate moods and emotions. Designed to detect non-verbal cues, including body language, facial expressions and tone of voice, technologies based on emotion AI are being developed by industries such as recruitment, health care and education.[2]

Generative AI: As earlier discussed in the section of the Major Ethical and Trust Issues in the Design, Development and Use of AI Applications and Data Management, another example is the variant of AI model called the generative AI based on Generative Pre-Trained Transformer (GPT – ChatGPT, AutoGPT) which is a large language model-based (LLM) chatbot developed by OpenAI and launched on November 30, 2022, and allows users to interact with it by using prompts or by asking questions represented in text and later in audio and visual formats.

Quantum AI: The combination of the capabilities of AI with quantum computing will result in an exponential speed of problem-solving and data processing far beyond the most advanced computer systems. This fertile area of deploying the power of quantum computing with the innovation of artificial intelligence (AI) accelerates the processing and modelling of vast amounts of complex datasets to generate outcomes far beyond human comprehension and ability.

Human-Centred Strategy for Humanising AI Applications

AI solution that is not subjected to robust ethical principles and practices, as discussed in this book, would portend significant, even life-threatening effects in industrial and societal contexts, as ethical methodologies for implementation and use of AI are necessary for safe, secure, reliable, resilient, functional and ethical systems.[3] The HAI book's approach to analysis and design provides a high-level overview of how to design, deploy, maintain, and decommission trustworthy technology for developers, owners, operators, and decision-makers in AI applications and ecosystems.

The analysis and design strategy also addresses various aspects of creating, acquiring, operationalising, maintaining, and decommissioning AI applications. It is to provide practical and actionable best practices for recognising, addressing, managing, and mitigating risks and their sources throughout the lifecycle of AI solutions that are developed in-house or acquired. The analysis and design approach is critical in achieving the goal of trustworthy AI that produces predictable and desirable business and operational outcomes, whereby all trustworthiness concerns must be addressed through architecture, design, and proper software implementation procedures.[4]

Human-Centric Principles and Practices in Design, Development and Deployment of Trustworthy AI Applications

One of the most important aspects of ethicising AI applications and services is adopting the human-centric design which cuts across all the domains of sociocultural, political, and economic domains of life. Together with relevant best practices, this approach would efficiently tackle the ethical challenges that come with the exponential changes and growth in the industry. The HCD (Human Centric Design), as it involves human perspectives, participation and engagement in the design, deployment, management, and maintenance of the solutions, also integrates periodic community oversight and feedback throughout the lifecycle of the solution. Major human-centric strategies and best practices for trustworthy AI solutions and use are as shown below (also detailed in Chapter 7):

Principles and Practices	Description
Humanising Artificial Intelligence (HAI)	The HAI is a practice model to educate, facilitate, and support multidiscipline and multicultural collaborations in humanising all aspects of AI innovations by instituting and incorporating sound human values, trustworthy standards and ethos into the design, development, deployment, and decommissioning of AI applications in the society. To humanise is to make a system trustworthy and friendly to humans. Humanising makes things more civilised, reasonable and trustworthy.
Participatory Research (PR)	The participatory research (PR) method encompasses research designs, methods, and frameworks that use systematic inquiry in co-creation and co-production arrangement with direct collaboration with those affected by the design, development, and use of the AI solution.[5] This is one of the ways to democratise the process of managing the entire lifecycle of AI applications from conception to decommissioning.
Multidisciplinary Consultations	A driving focus is ensuring that consultation and evaluation of AI applications are far-reaching and multi-disciplinary in stakeholder engagement. Gaining their insight and contributions is important throughout the lifecycle of the AI applications. The outcome of extensive consultations and joint decision-making activities with the stakeholders would be incorporated into the design, development and use of the AI application and be part of the lesson learned for future reference and use in the same process. Interests and stakeholders can be sourced from the public and private sectors, including governments, local authorities, commercial and non-commercial organisations, social partners, experts, academics, and citizens. This is further

Principles and Practices	Description
	discussed in the next section and the case study.
Consequence Scanning and Analysis	This is an Agile Practice for organisations to capture and analyse the potential consequences of their services and products on communities, people, and the planet.[6] This is further discussed in the next section and the case study.
Harms Modelling (Foundations of Assessing Harm)	Harms Modelling is a practice developed by Microsoft to help organisations expect potential harm and identify gaps in products and services that could expose people to risk. [7] This is further discussed in the next section and the case study.
EDI/B (Equality, Diversity, Inclusion and Belonging)	It aims to eradicate discrimination and bias based on a group or individual's protected characteristics. EDI (Equality, Diversity, and Inclusion) is a guideline for practices that ensure fair treatment and opportunity for all in society.[8] The EDIB (equality, diversity, inclusion, and belonging) encompasses a culture that develops and maintains fairness, celebrates differences, makes people feel valued and gives people a sense of belonging, being involved and integrated.
Data Privacy Impact Assessments (DPIAs) / Legitimate Interest Assessments	A DPIA[37] is a systematic and comprehensive way to analyse how data is processed and stored, helping organisations identify and minimise data protection risks.[9] Figure 3. 2: The Process Steps of Carrying Out a DPIA

Principles and Practices	Description
The WEF's Environmental, Social and Governance Reporting	Organisations, both private and public enterprises, are rethinking and redefining the metrics they use to define success well beyond profit and sales. This is in response to growing concerns among their employees, customers, investors, and impacted communities; many firms are making themselves accountable for their Environmental, Social, and Governance (ESG) practices.[10]
AI for Social Good (AI4SG) and the Seven Essential Factors	The AI4SG initiatives are successful in selected projects in helping reduce, mitigate, or eradicate a significant moral issue. Seven factors contribute to a successful design and deployment of socially good and responsible AI-based solutions; these are (1) falsifiability and incremental deployment; (2) safeguards against the manipulation of predictors; (3) receiver-contextualised intervention; (4) receiver-contextualised explanation and transparent purposes; (5) privacy protection and data subject consent; (6) situational fairness; and (7) human-friendly somatisation.[11]
Sustainable AI technology (Red AI Vs Green AI)	This is a new thinking and framework on the red AI (Artificial Intelligence) and green AI which seek to identify, define, advise, and advocate how the production, distribution, operation, and waste management of AI solutions can be managed with little or no impact on the environment.[12]
Unified Theory of Acceptance and Use of Technology (UTAUT)	The UTAUT2,[13] which is the extended model developed by Venkatesh et al. (2012) explains the objective and subjective factors that affect the acceptance and usage of Information and communications technology (ICT) like AI solutions by end users or consumers. It also echoes that an individual's intention to accept and use technology is determined by seven factors which are significant predictors of acceptance and use of the technology: (i) performance expectancy, (ii) effort expectancy, (iii) facilitating conditions, (iv) social influence, (v) hedonic motivation (vi) price value and (vii) habit.

Principles and Practices	Description
System and Operational Observability	Observability is a system management practice that goes beyond system monitoring as AI applications become more complex, ITOps (DevOps, DevSecOps, DataOps, MLOps, AIOps, DevEthOps, etc.), developers and management need better architectural and operational visibility into how the application stack and systems are running, their decision-making processes and outputs. Observability systems aid in better understanding and transparency of modern infrastructure and applications on what the real-time state is, who is affected, risk management, and issue resolution.
Public Awareness and Empowerment (Education, communication, consultation)	To win the public support and trust for the FRT and other solutions, the public needs to be empowered through appropriate and regular information sharing, education, consultation, and public communications like an approach developed by the Biometrics Institute[14] in using the Privacy Awareness Checklist (PAC) which encourages governments and private organisations to incorporate privacy awareness and training.[14]
Regulations, Public Oversight and Co-Creation	In building inclusive futures and protecting civil liberties in the design and implementation of ethical, legal, trusted, and inclusive digital services, there is a need to incorporate balanced and stringent regulations coupled with public oversight built on institutions of independent and impartial international multi-stakeholder bodies. It is worth noting that compliance, cooperation, and engagement should be secured through mutual respect and tolerance without weaponising shame, guilt, and blame to gain any form of cooperation.

Principles and Practices	Description
De-Weaponisation of Shame, Blame and Guilt	It is important to treat everyone fairly when using AI and other technologies. We should not use shame, blame, or guilt to make people feel wrong about their beliefs and culture. When people use these responses to humiliate and force others to comply, it becomes a problem. They become weapons that harm society and people's emotions, leading to anger, division, and community disintegration. These negative actions can happen unconsciously if not controlled, triggered by a situation or as subtle manipulation. However, as individuals and society, we must learn to use more constructive approaches and means of education, dialogue, regulation, empathy, and compromise in engendering change, compromise, and compliance. Ultimately, we should conduct our roles for the highest good of others, thereby driving and supporting the provision of fair, trusted and inclusive digital identity services necessary for sustainable, worldwide economic growth, prosperity, and equal opportunity for all.[15]

Table 4.1: List of Major Human-Centric Principles and Practices.

REFLECTION: AI AND SOCIAL LIFE

"*It is customary to offer a grain of comfort in the form of a statement that some peculiarly human characteristic could never be imitated by a machine. I cannot offer any such comfort, for I believe that no such bounds can be set.*"

- Alan Turing[Q3] (English Mathematician, Computer Scientist, Logician, Cryptanalyst, Philosopher, and Theoretical Biologist)

Personal Note:

MANAGING THE RISKS IN HUMAN-AI COLLABORATIONS

Empowerment or Disempowerment Adventure?

"I am ChatGPT. ... My main goal is to be a useful tool for people looking for information. I strive to provide accurate and helpful answers as best I can be based on my programming and training. ... I have no personal goals or motivations, as I am an artificial intelligence and have no consciousness or emotions. ... Inside me, I analyse the input I receive, break it down into its parts, and use algorithms to generate an answer based on the patterns and relationships I have learned from my training data. ... My training data consists of much text from various sources, such as books, articles, and websites" – ChatGPT ("Answer to prompts", August 4, 2023. Reference Chapter 3/No. 19)

This is the ChatGPT's answer to prompts that asked, "Who are you, what are your intentions, and how do you work?" In advancing AI/GenAI innovation and applications, people empowerment should be sacrosanct, and the applications should complement human rights, authority, and power to carry out or perform various acts or duties with autonomy and self-determination without inhibition or coercion. AI/GenAI applications should not be disempowering agents or means to deprive people of rights, power, authority, or influence, rendering them vulnerable, ineffectual, unimportant, or having no control over their lives and will to change.

Human-centric AI systems are potent tools for productive and transformative human-machine collaborations. They help to automate routine and repetitive tasks thereby freeing the workforce to focus on more creative and complex work. Workers are provided with real-time and clear insights by data analysis and visualisation, facilitating swift and quality decision-making, and helping them to improve their skills and performance. This approach of human-centric design and deployment of AI/GenAI aids human-machine collaboration with greater efficiency and productivity which may not be possible without AI technology.

Managing The Risks of Human-AI Collaborations

The necessity and proportionality of any AI application in its design, implementation and operationalisation require in-depth analyses of the associated barriers, enablers, and drivers of its design and use. The strategy of implementation adopted must close the gaps between principles and practices regarding ethical questions, ethics interpretations and applicability, and real-world operational practices as applied in different industries, sectors, and organisations.

Moreover, market and societal needs for AI solutions as main drivers may contend with unintended or intended barriers if robust and pragmatic ethical principles, laws, frameworks, and methodologies are not readily available in simple with easy-to-operate toolkits, such as this publication for suppliers (developers, deployers) and users alike. Based on experience in the field, a combination of conventional/waterfall and agile approaches in the implementation and operation of AI applications would go a long way in ensuring trust between manufacturers and end-users of the technology.

Democratising AI through Public Engagement

Based on the work we have done and data available in public engagement in the democratisation of AI, there is a need for concerted and sustainable effort to drive a systematic approach to making AI technologies, their awareness and understanding more accessible, affordable, and user-friendly for a broader range of users. This is regardless of their formal technology training, background, race, gender, demography, and belief. The main purpose of this engagement is to gather views and inputs from diverse communities, making their voices heard by manufacturers, policymakers, and other stakeholders alike.

A practical illustration of public and community engagement in AI involved a sponsored partnership program by academic institutions and UK government agencies as one of their flagship projects to empower researchers to engage and empower marginalised communities. These communities include the homeless, vulnerable families and local communities co-opted in delivering public engagement activities around ethical Artificial Intelligence and data-driven technologies. This would undoubtedly enable traditionally marginalised communities to have a voice in the field. A group of data scientists and AI researchers, known as Public Engagement Ambassadors (PEAs), are trained and mentored in the methodologies of democratisation of AI through co-creation, co-production, and co-ownership of AI applications with local communities in Levenshulme and Tatton in the UK.[1]

Tools for Risk and Impact Assessment of AI Applications

As part of the operationalisation tactics to achieve a trustworthy AI application from the technical and human requirements, one of the main steps in this direction is to expect and understand the impact of the AI application from concept to commercialisation or to use on all the stakeholders. Therefore, the impact assessment using the tools shown below and the case study section in this book are valuable highlights.

Consequence Scanning for Impact Assessment

This analysis aims to perform consequence scanning on an AI trustworthiness. This is by identifying the intended and unintended consequences of AI applications and solutions from the point of view of all stakeholders. It is then to suggest how negative consequences should be identified and mitigated. For example, the table below shows a consequence scanning template on AI-based face recognition technology, which is also discussed in detail in the case study section of this book. This is also thoroughly discussed and analysed in the case study section of bias in and bias out.

Name of AI Application:	Name of AI Application	Reference	State reference number	Year	Date in year
Brief description of your selected application	Description of AI-Application and primary function				
Who are the stakeholders?	As stated below: - Project Supplier: Project Stakeholder(s):. Target User(s): Beneficiaries:				
What are the intended and unintended consequences of this AI application?	List Intended Consequences: List Unintended Consequences:				
What are the positive consequences of this AI application?	List the functional benefits of the use of the AI application.				
What are the consequences we want to mitigate?	List the known risks and potential issues that need to be addressed.				

Table 5.2: Consequence Scanning[2] Template

Harms Modelling for Impact Assessment

Harms Modelling is a practice developed by Microsoft to help organisations anticipate potential harm and identify gaps in products and services that could expose people and organisations to risk. The table below is developed as a practical example to analyse or model an online interactive audit tool for AI solutions and intended stakeholders in the light of potential risks and threats that exist without proper toolkits to mitigate and control them.[3] More detail is discussed later in the book in the case study section.

Impact Assessment Report Analyses of Consequence Scanning and Harms Modelling

As shown and discussed in the case study section of this book, both consequence scanning and harm modelling help anticipate the risks involved in designing and rolling out an AI-based solution. As seen above, whilst the consequence scanning helped to have a deeper understanding of the stakeholders, the potential benefits (pros) and potential drawbacks (cons) of AI-based solution deployment, the harms modelling of the solution's usage gave a deeper understanding of the severity, scope, scale, probability, and frequency of the potential harms unethical AI solution can have on the well-being of human and society.

Both tools are crucial in proactively enabling, educating, and preparing the manufacturers, designers, developers, engineers, policymakers, and other stakeholders (as listed in the consequence scanning section) in the lifecycle of AI-based solutions as the solutions are deployed in society. All stakeholders are aware, educated and prepared about the potential risks and to put measures in place to prevent, mitigate and resolve any attendant issues or problems that may arise.

Risk Assessment and Management of Trustworthy AI Applications

According to the EU's Regulatory Framework on AI called *The Artificial Intelligence Act,*[4] the AI-associated sociotechnical risk factors of design, deployment, and use with their varying probability of occurrence and severity is related to all human domains (social, political, economic, environmental, moral, ethical, cultural, and legal).

To properly monitor and control identified risks as identified using both consequence scanning and harm modelling, the risk management plan of using the risk matrix and risk register helps to manage the risks and threats throughout the lifecycle of the solution, ensuring strong governance and oversight in the management of the solution from conceptualisation, analysis, design, development, deployment and use as they impact different aspects of the life of identified stakeholders.

The Risk Matrix

The risk matrix applies to sociotechnical domains and factors of social, moral, cultural, environmental, legal, political, economic, etc. A typical example is shown below, depicting the various degrees of likelihood of occurrence and impact on identified stakeholders.

Risk Domain		Consequence of Failure (Severity)				
People		Slight Injury	Minor Injury	Major	Single Fatality	Multiple Fatalities
Asset		Slight Damage	Minor Damage	Local Damage	Major Damage	Extensive Damage
Environment		Slight Effect	Minor Effect	Localised Effect	Major Effect	Massive Effect
Reputation		Slight Impact	Local Impact	Industry Impact	National Impact	International Impact
Ranking		1 = Negligible	2 = Minor	3 = Moderate	4 = Major	5 = Catastrophic
Probability of Failure (Likelihood)	A = Very likely to happen	Medium	High	High	Very High	Very High
	B = Likely to happen	Low	Moderate	High	High	Very High
	C = Possible to happen	Low	Low	Moderate	High	High
	D = Unlikely to happen	Very Low	Low	Low	Moderate	High
	E = Very unlikely to happen	Very Low	Very Low	Low	Low	Moderate

Table 5.2: Risk Matrix of Trustworthy Artificial Intelligence

The Risk Register and Report

Based on the risk matrix above, a sample of the risk assessment register and status (report) showing the list of identified major and critical risk factors, sociotechnical domains, their control measures, schedule, and status is shown below.

Ref	Identified Major Risk	Those Likely To Be Affected	Risk Matrix Rating	Risk Control and Mitigating Action (Measure)	Responsible	Date To Carried Out Control and Mitigation	Status
1.0	Threat to individual and societal privacy		(State rating)				
2.0	Infringement of personal freedoms (sample)	(State organisation and user)		State action	State names	State the date of the control measure	State status
3.0	Violation of personal rights						
4.0	Data vulnerabilities (sample)	(State organisation and user)		State action	State names	State the date of the control measure	State status
5.0	Fraudulent and criminal tools						
6.0	Imperfect technology (sample)	(State organisation and user)	(State rating)	State action	State names	State the date of the control measure	State status
7.0	Exploitation and manipulation of data and system		(State rating)				

Table 5.3: Risk Assessment Register of Trustworthy Artificial Intelligence

Ethics Assurance (EA) And Ethic Control (EC) in the Design, Development and Deployment of Trustworthy Artificial Intelligence

Ethics Assurance in the design, development, and deployment of AI applications and data management focuses on the procedures and processes to improve the standards or criteria of trustworthiness, as stated earlier. It is also to ensure compliance with guidelines and requirements of ethics regulatory bodies as desired or recommended in the design, development, and use of the solution. These EA processes and procedures include periodic (weekly) reviews, multidisciplinary consultations, training, audits, and requisite documentation systems as described in preceding sections.

Ethics Control (EC) is identifying and detecting deviations or defects that impact the standards or criteria of trustworthiness during and after the design, development, and deployment of AI applications and data management. Also, EC processes and procedures help monitor and verify that the deliverables, features, functions, and operations of AI applications and data continually and consistently meet defined trustworthy standards and specifications.

REFLECTION: AI AND ECONOMICS

> *"There will be two kinds of companies at the end of this decade: those that are fully utilising AI, and those that are out of business."*
>
> - Peter H. Diamandis[Q5] (A Serial Entrepreneur, Futurist, Technologist, Bestselling Author)

Personal Note:

ORGANIZATION READINESS FOR HUMANISING AI APPLICATIONS

Ethics Standards of Humanising AI Applications

The standards, criteria, and requirements for humanising AI applications incorporate ethics and trustworthy qualities into the design, development, deployment and lifecycle management of the AI systems. These humanisation standards or requirements are non-functional specifications whose qualitative and quantitative degrees are what the system or solutions must fulfil and satisfy under the lawful, ethical, and technical requirements per global guidelines, rules, and regulations.

Based on decades of work with industry leaders and helping organisations shape strategy and operation for growth and efficiency, it is noted that sponsorship, organisational structure, and governance go a long way to determine the success of any initiative like ethics and governance of humanising AI applications in an organisation. The list of standards and criteria listed in this book are uniquely categorised into major criteria or standards (organisational readiness, technology, legal and ethical). The organisational readiness requirement is incorporated to understand and capture the influence of organisational approach and culture on the success of developing strategy and managing operations of ethics and governance of AI application in any organisation.

Ethics Intelligence in Humanising AI Applications

Ethics intelligent organisations and professionals know how their strategy and operational transaction influence and impact others and society. Ethically intelligent organisation knows how to apply and use this awareness to be thoughtful, responsible, transparent, people-centred, and planet-sustainable. Ethics intelligence and its assurance are crucial to any organisation in this age as they are key sustainability and performance indicators which underpin the practice that organisations and professionals know what is right and are committed and courageous to do what is right.

The different ethics standards are uniquely discussed in this book, where organisational readiness for ethics governance is incorporated with ethical technology and legal requirements, are detailed and practical in developing and maintaining a high maturity level of any organisation's ethics intelligence. This high maturity level as a measure of ethics IQ (intelligence quotient) of the organisation is a trademark for business success, resilience, and trustworthiness among stakeholders, customers, partners, and society. An organisation-wide approach to assessing and measuring ethics intelligence in humanising AI helps create and sustain a fair, accountable, transparent leadership and organisational management culture.

In the disruptive and hypercompetitive world of today's marketplace, charting a resilient course for success requires robust ethical standards that build and support trustworthiness and healthy relationships with the public and all stakeholders. Ethics intelligence, when operationalised in humanising AI applications, focuses on how healthy ethics principles and practices are woven into the organisational fabrics, managing them to be more than ticking the boxes but tools and mindsets to help organisational leaders and professionals turn theory into actions that create sustained outcomes which drive positive values and growth for the benefit of all stakeholders, the society and posterity.

Organisational Readiness for Ethics and Governance of AI Applications

These are standards (roles, processes, and attributes) of the practices in the organisation, which are scored and ranked at different weights and are required to support the design, development, and use of trustworthy AI applications successfully in the organisation. These practices, attributes and roles are Strategy, Leadership (Governance), Personnel, Finance (Budget), Methodology, Education, Plan (Structure), Practice (Operations) etc.

Measuring your Organisational Readiness for Ethics and Governance of AI

One of the best indicators to help organisations determine whether they are ready or headed down the path of ensuring the design, development and use of AI applications is ethical, and position them with the right capability to manage AI applications effectively and efficiently, is to assess whether they have an environment that supports major ethics organisational readiness criteria/standards as stated below (please note that this list is not exhaustive). The assessment measures whether the workforce (employees and senior management), partners and other stakeholders are informed and empowered with ethics and governance of AI and have the knowledge, tools, and organisational support to strategise, operationalise and manage AI applications and their lifecycle.

The following list is developed based on research and consulting works that have been done to help determine your organisation's readiness, educate or create awareness and show specific organisational areas to be set up or improved to create and sustain ethical and sustainable organisation.

Organisational Readiness Standards/Criteria for Ethics of AI Applications

Organisational Readiness Domain	Description	Ethics Practice	Score (1 to 5)
Strategy	A plan of action designed to achieve a long-term or overall aim. It is a general plan or set of plans intended to achieve something, especially over a long period of time.	The organisation's clear vision, aims and objectives for the adoption and use of trustworthy AI applications, toolkits, and practice in the organisation.	
Leadership	Leadership is the ability of an individual or a group of people to influence and guide followers or members of an organisation, society, or team. Leadership is a process of social influence that maximises the efforts of others towards the achievement of a goal.	The committed and structured leadership for direction in the adoption and use of trustworthy AI applications, toolkits, and practices in the organisation	

Organisational Readiness Domain	Description	Ethics Practice	Score (1 to 5)
Process	This is a collection of linked tasks that find their end in delivering a service or product to a client. A business process has also been defined as a set of activities and tasks that, once completed, will accomplish an organisational goal.	Effective and inclusive execution of globally accepted processes in the implementation, adoption, and operation of trustworthy AI applications and toolkits and practice	
Governance	Corporate governance is the system of rules, practices, and processes by which a company is directed and controlled. Corporate Governance refers to how companies are governed and for what purpose. It identifies who has power and accountability, and who decides.	The committed and continuous monitoring, and control structure of the organisation towards the adoption and use of trustworthy AI applications, toolkits, and practices in the organisation	

Organisational Readiness Domain	Description	Ethics Practice	Score (1 to 5)
Learning (Awareness and Education)	Business learning includes the development of knowledge about various aspects of business, including regulations, best practices, and necessary skills for success.	The level of information (knowledge), understanding and skills to implement, adopt, and operate trustworthy AI applications, toolkits, and practice	
Operational Practice	Operations management is the administration of business practices to create the highest level of efficiency possible within an organisation. This is also the practice of handling day-to-day business functions in a manner that is efficient and that maximises profitability.	The measure of the outcome of operating (operationalising) trustworthy AI applications, toolkits, and practice in the organisation.	
Organisational Culture	It is the sum of your formal and informal systems	Organisational receptiveness to change regarding	

Organisational Readiness Domain	Description	Ethics Practice	Score (1 to 5)
	behaviours and values, all of which create an experience for your employees and customers. At its core, company culture is how things get done around the workplace. Business culture refers to the set of behavioural and procedural norms that can be observed within a company. Organisational culture refers to the values, beliefs, and behaviours that determine how a company's employees and management interact, perform, and handle business transactions. Often, corporate culture is implied, not	implementing and operating trustworthy AI applications, toolkits, and practice.	

Organisational Readiness Domain	Description	Ethics Practice	Score (1 to 5)
	defined, and develops organically over time from the cumulative traits of the people that the company hires.		
Total Score (Unit)			
Total Percentage (%) = ((Total Score/35) x100%)			

Table 6.1: Organisational Readiness Criteria for Ethics of AI Applications

Scoring the Organisational Readiness Standards/Criteria

This is how to interpret the assessment score based on the above using the Likert Scales[1,] which is widely used in social and educational research. Consideration is given to categories of response (values in the scale), size of the scale (1 to 5), the direction of the scale (low to high), the ordinal nature of Likert-derived data, and appropriate statistical analysis of such data. Likert scales fall within the ordinal level of measurement: the categories of response have directionality, but the intervals between them cannot be presumed equal.

The percentage of the sum of each score of these standards or criteria indicates where your organisation stands in the effective management and operation of ethics and governance of AI applications.

Score Range	Organisational Readiness Level and Indication
0 – 45%	Here, the percentage of the total organisational readiness criteria or standards is equal or within the range as specified (x ≤ 0 – 45%); this shows that the organisation does not have the capability required to effectively manage and operate the ethics and governance of AI applications.
46% - 75%	Here, there is a partial form of accountability which incorporates an effective governance and oversight process of AI ethics. It is important to ensure that the objectives of the standards are fulfilled. The percentage of the total sum of the organisational readiness criteria or standards is equal or within the range as specified (x ≤ 46 – 75%); this indicates that the organisation has partial capability required to effectively manage and operate the ethics and governance of AI applications.
76% - 100%	Here, there is a strong form of accountability and governance which incorporates an effective oversight process of AI ethics, and it is important to ensure that the objectives of the standards are fulfilled. The percentage of the total organisational readiness criteria or standards is equal or within the range, as specified (x ≤ 76 – 100%); this indicates that the organisation has strong capability and organisational tools required to effectively and sustainably manage and operate the ethics and governance of AI applications.

Table 6.2: Organisational Readiness Scoring and Ranking for Ethics of AI Applications

The assessment and scoring above on behalf of the entire organisation only give a self-diagnostic of how well an organisation is performing in the ethics and governance of AI applications. On a more expansive scale, to gain a more accurate understanding, it is recommended that the survey be administered to a representative sample (employees, senior management, and partners) of your organisation, across levels and departments. It is after this organisation-wide assessment that deductions and conclusions can be drawn as per the areas to improve and maximise based on strengths, weaknesses, threats, and opportunities associated with the corresponding organisational readiness level.

Technological Standards or Criteria for Ethics of AI Applications

These are standards (capabilities and attributes) of the quality of the AI technology services and products, which are scored and ranked in different weights and are required to successfully support the design, development, and use of trustworthy AI applications in any organisation. These technology attributes include Acceptability, Simplicity, Administration, Robustness, Security, Safety, Expertise, Privacy, Piracy, Warranty, Lawfulness, Explainability, Traceability, Cost, Inclusivity in Design, Diversity in Design, Multicultural Design, etc.

Technology Standards/Criteria for Ethics of AI Applications

The list below is not exhaustive, and the domains are not mutually exclusive. They are to serve as a guide in evaluating and gauging the technology requirements/criteria for ethics of AI applications and as they apply to different levels or degrees of quality of ethical practice:

Technology Standards/Criteria Domain	Description
Acceptability	The quality of being accepted; the quality of being satisfactory and able to be agreed to or approved of; the degree to which something is agreed or approved by most people in a society.
Simplicity	The quality or condition of being plain or uncomplicated in form or design; the quality or condition of being easy to understand or do.
Robustness	The property of being strong and healthy in the constitution, the ability to withstand or overcome adverse conditions or rigorous testing. The quality of being strong, healthy or unlikely to break or fail.
Security	An act and process concerned with protecting against intentional harm caused by external factors, e.g. cyberattacks, theft, unauthorised access to organisational assets in the use of AI applications. This maintains the integrity and confidentiality of sensitive information. Also, security stands for crime prevention by using AI applications.
Safety	The act and process in the design, development and deployment of AI applications focusing on preventing

Technology Standards/Criteria Domain	Description
	unintentional harm and physical hazards, such as accidents or natural disasters relating to the use of AI. Also, safety stands for accident avoidance because of the use of AI applications.
Administration	The process or activity of running a business, organisation, the arrangements, and tasks needed to control the operation of a plan or organisation/activities involved in managing an organisation;
Interoperability	Interoperability is the capability of an AI application or system to work or connect with other applications or systems. Also, AI systems or software can exchange and use information from other systems or software.
Learning and Expertise	The acquisition of knowledge or skills through study, experience, or being taught. Also, acquiring new understanding, knowledge, behaviours, skills, values, attitudes, and preferences
Openness	The quality of being receptive to new ideas, opinions, or arguments. Also, the key attributes that counter obstructions to business success and improve collaboration, information, and technology workflows.
Privacy	The practice in the design, development, and deployment of AI applications that does not violate individual rights. It allows individuals to determine when, how, and to what extent personal information about them is shared with or communicated.
Piracy	The practice in the design, development, and deployment of AI applications that does not encourage or involve the unauthorised use or reproduction of other people's work. This refers to the unauthorised duplication of copyrighted

Technology Standards/Criteria Domain	Description
	content sold at substantially lower prices in the 'grey' market.
Warranty	A written guarantee issued to the purchaser of an AI application by its manufacturer, promising to repair or replace it within a specified period.
Lawfulness	An essential and distinguishing attribute of AI applications' design, development and deployment conforming to or under the law of any sort (such as natural, divine, common, or canon).
Explainability and Observability	This ensures that AI is designed and deployed for humans to easily detect, interpret, and understand its decision process. It is also a process to reduce and mitigate an AI application's lack of transparency.
Traceability	The practice in the design, development, and deployment of AI applications with means to verify their history, location, and use by documented or recorded identification. The quality of having an origin or course of development that may be found or followed.
Reliability	The ability of AI applications to function under stated conditions for a specified time
Availability	The assurance that an AI application has suitable recoverability and protection from system failures, natural disasters, or malicious attacks.
Maintainability	Maintainability is the probability of performing a successful repair action at a time on AI applications. In other words, maintainability measures the ease and speed with which an AI application can be restored to operational status after a failure occurs.

Technology Standards/Criteria Domain	Description
Usability	The practice in the design, development, and deployment of AI applications to provide easy-to-use conditions for end users to perform tasks safely, effectively, and efficiently.
Compatibility	Compatibility of an AI application ensures interoperability between it and other technology applications and solutions of the same or different types or different versions. AI compatibility means programs, devices, and systems interact seamlessly regardless of manufacturers and geography.
Portability	The usability of the same AI application and software in different environments. A characteristic attributed to an AI application is that it can run with minimal modification on operating systems other than the one for which it was developed. It is the generalised abstraction between AI application logic and system interfaces.
Expandability	The ability of an AI application to accommodate enhancements to its capacity or capabilities. Also, the ability to increase capability while retaining or increasing response time and throughout performance.
Internationalisation	The design, development, and deployment of AI applications for users worldwide with different languages, functional requirements and user interfaces. Also, AI designs that meet the needs of different countries and can be easily adapted.
Inclusivity in Design	Digital inclusion involves AI applications enabling and supporting fair access to and use of information and communication technologies for participation in social and economic life, including education, social services, health, and community

Technology Standards/Criteria Domain	Description
	participation. This designing AI to enable equitable, meaningful, and safe access to opportunities.
Diversity in Design	Diversity in design means using AI to enable and support the diversity of experience, perspective, and creativity — otherwise known as diversity of thought — and these can be diverse cultural perspectives that inspire creativity and drive innovation.
Multicultural Design	The practice of designing AI for cross-cultural considerations which encompasses tailoring and adapting design elements, such as images, colour, and layouts, to support the cultural (beliefs, arts, laws, customs, etc.) needs of customers and businesses.
Regulation	This refers to the range of regulatory tools that governments, regulators, businesses, and other bodies use to manage the impact of AI applications' design, development, deployment, and decommissioning in society.

Table 6.3: Technology Standard Criteria for Ethics of AI Applications

The assessment and scoring of the above on behalf of the entire organisation only give a self-diagnostic of how well an organisation performs in humanising AI through AI ethics and governance regarding the design, development, deployment, and lifecycle management. For deeper evaluation and diagnosis, it is suggested to survey a representative sample of your organisation's employees, senior management, and partners across different levels and departments. This approach will help determine where to improve or maximise based on strengths, weaknesses, threats, and opportunities associated with AI technology standards.

Legal and Ethical Standards for Ethics and Governance of AI Applications

These are joint standards (qualities, roles, processes, policies, and attributes) of the practices in the organisation, which are scored and ranked in different weights and are required to successfully support the design, development, and use of trustworthy AI applications in the organisation. These practices, attributes, processes, and roles include Security, Safety, Fairness, Transparency, Accountability, Governance, Expertise, Privacy, Piracy, Warranty, Lawfulness, Explainability, Traceability, Sustainability, Redress, Trade-offs, Education, Consultation, Diversity, Inclusivity, Oversight, etc.

Legal and Ethical Standards/Criteria for Ethics AI Application

The list below is not exhaustive, and the domains are not mutually exclusive as they apply to different levels or degrees of quality of ethical practice:

Legal and Ethical Standards/Criteria Domain	Description
Security	Security is a measure of protection from crime, violence, or other harm due to AI applications. It also involves protection and

Legal and Ethical Standards/Criteria Domain	Description
	measures against deliberate (intentional) potential threats that may arise from the design, development, and use of AI applications.
Safety	Safety focuses on protection against unintentional threats, especially physical harms, that may arise from the design, development, and use of AI applications.
Fairness	This upholds fairness in the design, development, and deployment of AI in making judgments and decisions that are free from discrimination and bias. The quality of treating people fairly and reasonably.
Transparency	As an ethic that spans science, engineering, business, and the humanities, transparency is operating in such a way that it is easy for others to see what actions are performed. The quality of making the design, development and use of AI applications open to public or authorised agencies.
Accountability	In terms of ethics and governance, accountability is equated with answerability, blameworthiness, liability, and the expectation of account-giving. Being responsible for and able to give a satisfactory reason for the design, development, and use of AI applications.
Governance	The process of making and enforcing decisions within an organisation or society, Aso, the act or process of governing or overseeing the control and direction of design, development, and use of AI applications.
Expertise	Special skill or knowledge that is gained by training, study, or practice. A high level of skill or knowledge gained in the design, development, and use of AI applications.

Legal and Ethical Standards/Criteria Domain	Description
Privacy	The right to keep one's personal information and data without breach and violation by the design, development, and use of AI applications.
Piracy	The unauthorised use or reproduction of other people's work in the design, development, and use of AI applications.
Copyright	The practice in the design, development, and deployment of AI applications that respects intellectual property that gives its owner the exclusive right to copy, distribute, adapt, display, and perform a creative work. It helps protect the creator of the original material so that no one can duplicate or use it without consent from the original owner.
Warranty	A written guarantee is issued to the purchaser of an AI application by its manufacturer, promising to repair or replace it within a specified period.
Lawfulness	The practice in the design, development, and deployment of AI applications as allowed or permitted by law and not contrary to lawful enterprise. They are recognised and sanctioned by law.
Explainability or Interpretability	The quality possessed by AI applications that can be explained and understood. Also, the concept that an AI machine learning model and its output can be explained in a way that "makes sense" to a human being at an acceptable level.
Traceability	The practice in the design, development, and deployment of AI applications with means to verify their history, location, and use by documented or recorded identification. The quality of having an origin or course of development that may be found or followed
Sustainability	The practice in the design, development, and deployment of AI applications with the ability to be maintained at a specific rate or

Legal and Ethical Standards/Criteria Domain	Description
	level. Also, it is a social goal where AI applications enable and support people's ability to co-exist on earth over time without the depletion of natural resources that maintain ecological balance.
Redress	The practice in the design, development, and deployment of AI applications with the remedy or measure to set right an undesirable or unfair situation. Redress implies making compensation or reparation for an unfairness, injustice, or imbalance.
Trade-offs	The practice in the design, development, and deployment of AI applications which enables and supports reasonable compromise. Also, balancing of factors, all of which are not attainable simultaneously.
Learning and Education	The practice in the design, development, and deployment of AI applications which enables and supports the act and effort of spreading information, knowledge, and skills. The aims are to empower others, create awareness in decision-making, and improve others' understanding of AI.
Consultation	The practice in the design, development, and deployment of AI applications which enables and involves communication participation and engagement of all relevant stakeholders.
Diversity	The practice in the design, development, and deployment of AI applications which enables and supports the representation and empowerment of people of different socio-cultural factors such as age, gender, ethnicity, religion, disability, sexual orientation, education, and national origin.
Inclusivity	The practice in the design, development, and deployment of AI applications which supports how well different people's contributions, presence and perspectives are

Legal and Ethical Standards/Criteria Domain	Description
	valued and integrated into an environment or course.
Oversight	Oversight is the actions and measures taken to review and monitor AI applications' design, development, and use to ensure they achieve expected results for the benefit of society.
Internationalisation	The practice of design and use of AI applications, products and services to meet the regulatory requirements and needs of international markets of different languages, cultures, and geographies.

Table 6.4: Legal and Ethical Standards/Criteria for Ethics of AI Applications

The assessment and scoring of the above on behalf of the entire organisation only give a self-diagnostic of how well an organisation is performing in the legal and ethical standards of humanising AI applications. On a more expansive scale, to gain a more accurate understanding, it is recommended that the survey be administered to a representative sample (employees, senior management, and partners) of your organisation, across levels and departments. It is after this organisation-wide assessment that deductions and conclusions can be drawn as per the areas to improve and maximise based on strengths, weaknesses, threats, and opportunities associated with the corresponding technology standards in ethics and governance of AI applications.

Quantitative and Qualitative Assessment/Audit of Ethics of AI

Continuous data-driven and evidence-based assessment or audit of any organisation in the maturity of the ethics and governance of AI are highly recommended for better understanding, accuracy and objectivity of their readiness and trustworthiness in their relationships and interaction with the public. As contained in this chapter, the quantitative assessment/audit of measurement should be complemented with a qualitative assessment/audit. This qualitative assessment, which includes real-life interviews, reviews of documentation and artefacts, case studies review, questionnaires, first-hand observation, meeting with focus groups, participant observation, audio and video recordings, etc., helps to shed light on other unwritten factors of influence and perceptions of the state of ethics. A qualitative audit further solidifies the objective result of the exercise for greater reliability.

Considering the germane point that AI governance and ethics have become a global phenomenon, the approach, methodology, guideline, regulation, standards, and toolkits employed in the assessment and measurement of this practice should be robust with such capabilities and capacities that could help ethics professional, and stakeholders alike navigate the murky rivers of its inherent risks and issues.

REFLECTION: AI AND LEGALITY

> *"It's dangerous when it works and even more dangerous when it doesn't work."*
>
> - Robert William[27] *(The first person to be wrongfully arrested in 2020 due to the use of AI-based facial recognition technology)*

Personal Note:

CASE STUDIES: BIAS IN, BIAS OUT

Digital Capitalism and Dictatorship: Profit, Power, and People's Priorities

New frontiers in AI and emerging technologies are transforming our lives and livelihood, dictating how we live and work. These emerging technologies being introduced or are already in use in various sectors of society are the ones to watch; these are AI-enabled applications from facial recognition technologies (FRTs), drug discovery AI, generative AIs (ChatGPT, AutoGPT, xGPT, etc.), deepfakes, and quantum AI in studying emotional intelligence. Advancements in these applications have tremendous existential implications for the future of humanity.

Face recognition solutions have been the subject of research and debate over the years and have been used in countless applications in many areas of life. Facial recognition technology (FRT) is one of the major biometric identification technologies applied in different fields involving security, e-commerce, economics, and the military. It is a touchless identification application which detects and applies irreplaceable or unique logic or rules to users using their iris recognition and other unique facial attributes as data features to train an artificial intelligence system for real-time face detection and recognition.

The key ethical issues and data governance procedures that are germane to humanising an AI-based application like facial recognition technology (FRT) for the common good of society need to be discussed in practical terms. As stated in the previous sections, the approach follows a sequence of proven thoughts stating ethical issues and data governance practices, then highlights the current ethical guidelines, frameworks, principles, and legislation.

In humanising AI-based FRT, all-round impact assessments and analyses need to be carried out on the sociotechnical characteristics of how humans interact with the technology regarding social, moral, cultural, political, economic, legal, and ethical issues. The following sections highlight attendant ethical problems and discuss essential tools, processes, and best practices to resolve, mitigate and manage them by designers, developers, engineers, manufacturers, policymakers, civil societies, and the public in general.

Algorithm Bias Against People's Privacy, Privilege and Positionality

Michael Oliver, of Detroit, Michigan, was driving to work in July 2019 when he was pulled over, arrested, and charged with felony theft in connection with an incident in which someone else had reached into a car, grabbed someone's phone, and threw it. He was held in police custody for three days before being let go, and the charges were dropped against him two weeks later.[1 2.]

Nijeer Parks of Paterson, New Jersey, had never even set foot in Woodbridge when his grandmother called him in January 2019 to tell him that the Woodbridge police had a warrant out for his arrest. He got a ride to Woodbridge to clear up what he thought was a mistake, only to find himself arrested, charged with a crime, and held at the county jail for ten days, including four days in intake, isolated from other people. He spent ten months working to clear his name before the charges against him were finally dropped on the night before he would have gone to trial.[12]

Robert Williams, of Farmington Hills, Michigan, had just arrived home from work in January 2020 when two Detroit police officers approached him in his driveway and arrested him in front of his wife and two young daughters for a 2018 shoplifting incident in a store that Mr Williams had only been to once, in 2014. He was detained for thirty hours and forced to sleep on the floor of an overcrowded cell before he was released on a personal bond. The charges were then dropped against him, but he and his family were traumatised by the incident. His daughters took up playing games involving arresting people and have accused Robert of stealing things.[12]

These three cases of mistaken identity followed the same pattern. In all three cases, law enforcement representatives had an image of a perpetrator, used face recognition software to search for people whose faces resembled that image, developed a lead based on the search results, confirmed their lead with the help of eyewitness identification, and then made an arrest. In all three cases, face recognition technology directed law enforcement representatives to the wrong suspect, and eyewitnesses erroneously confirmed the mistaken identification. This pattern raises an important question: Does law enforcement use of face recognition technology increase the likelihood of erroneous eyewitness identifications and, ultimately, of wrongful convictions in U.S. criminal law due to differences in social position and power that shape identities and access in society?[12]

Integrated Analysis of the Social, Moral, Cultural, Environmental, Legal, Economic, Political, and Ethical Issues of AI-based Facial Recognition Technology (FRT)

Law enforcement agencies need to address inherent limitations and concerns in the deployment of real-time and AI-based facial recognition technology (FRT). The potential problems are majorly in the areas of errors and biases, which have enormous ramifications for society and the reputation of the governmental agency involved. AI algorithms have a probabilistic guarantee of accuracy when dealing with structured and unstructured datasets, and coupled with intentional and unintentional biases, these technical limitations make up the multifaceted issues of the policing FRT.[3]

The momentum for facial recognition usage for policing, domestic, and health relating to COVID-19 exposure and tracking has seemed to wane over the past year and a half.[4] So also is the need to implement robust oversight and regulations on its use in society in ways that are unbiased, responsible, accountable, fair, transparent, and ethical. The analyses of the global ramifications of the risks and issues of facial recognition and policing concerning social, moral, cultural, environmental, economic, legal, and ethical domains are the main thrusts of this report.

These challenges, which stem from bias and inconsistent outcomes coupled with blurry regulatory rules around facial recognition and policing, remain a big concern. In the USA, Amazon, Microsoft, and IBM announced in 2022 that they would halt the sale of facial recognition software to police departments and called for federal regulation of the technology. Whilst Congress has passed no laws regulating police use of facial recognition in the year since, privacy and civil liberties advocates said the cessation of the rollout of this technology as recommended by some big tech companies is a promising first step, but they remain concerned that some tech companies continue to profit from surveillance tools used by police.[4] To analyse and discuss the various issues with their attendant limitation and concerns, and how they affect all societal stakeholders, these are the dominant challenges.

Social Issues of Facial Recognition Technology

Research has long shown that facial recognition software may incorporate accidental racial and gender bias. According to a paper co-authored by MIT computer scientist Joy Buolamwini and renowned AI researcher Timnit Gebru,[5] it was shown that the outcome of IBM and Microsoft's facial recognition systems were significantly worse for identifying darker-skinned individuals. Studies by the American Civil Liberties Union and M.I.T.[6] found that Amazon's *Rekognition* technology misidentifies women and people of colour more frequently than it does white men.

Evaluating three commercial gender classification systems using a balanced dataset shows that darker-skinned females are the most misclassified group (with error rates of up to 34.7%). The maximum error rate for lighter-skinned males is 0.8%. The substantial disparities in the accuracy of classifying darker females, lighter females, darker males, and lighter males in gender classification systems require urgent attention if commercial companies are to build genuinely fair, transparent, and accountable facial analysis algorithms.[6]

However, in recent times, based on improved skills and a deeper understanding of facial nuances, facial recognition technology (FRT) has been adapted for another social angle such as identity recognition and locating missing persons in war zones. A clear example is the recent news about Clearview AI, a private American AI firm, assisting the Ukrainian government in the ongoing war. Clearview AI scrapes billions of images from social media sites such as Twitter, Facebook, and Instagram to build a search engine for facial images. Someone with Clearview AI's technology can upload an image which Clearview AI's FRT can then compare to the billions of images in the Clearview AI database, confirming identity.[7]

Moral Issues of Facial Recognition Technology

A moral issue in using FRT by law enforcement agencies can be understood as having the potential to cause psychological and physiological harm or discomfort to any member of the society regardless of race, gender orientation and nationality. This moral issue can be resolved by considering the technical component and keeping moral values in mind by individuals in these agencies. The services rendered by the law enforcement's FRT must be generally accepted as honest, impartial, and fair, promoting equity, public safety, health, and welfare.[8]

Many professional associations and government agencies, especially in law enforcement, have proposed different codes of ethics to guide acceptable moral expressions by their members in the operations of FRT and in fulfilling their professional duties; the fundamentals of these codes of ethics, as earlier stated, are used to enforce strict adherence in the four major areas of use of the policing FRT which are *Stop and Identify*, *Arrest and Identify*, *Investigate and Identify*, and *Real-time Video Surveillance*. In all these areas of use, the individuals in these agencies are urged to uphold moral leadership and moral responsibility within ethical limits:[8]

Moral Leadership

The members of the law enforcement agency are encouraged to take responsibility for providing and operating the FRT. This moral leadership role can be understood as success when an individual collectively moves a group towards making the FRT services ethical and trustworthy to the populace. As moral leaders, they are to direct, motivate, organise, creatively manage, or, in other ways, move groups towards achieving and maintaining the codes of conduct in the operation of the FRT.

Moral Responsibility

The responsibilities of law enforcement agencies, if not taken properly, result in adverse effects on the well-being of society. The individuals in these agencies are expected to act responsibly in performing their duties. They are expected to ensure members adhere to and fulfil professional duties in using the FRT. These responsibilities include holding paramount the safety, health, and welfare of the public and conducting themselves honourably, responsibly, ethically, and lawfully to enhance the honour, reputation, and usefulness of the profession in using the policing FRT.[9]

Cultural Issues of Facial Recognition Technology

The recent national surveys of the values and beliefs of people in the countries that are members of the World Values Survey Association (WVSA),[10] which is a non-profit organisation funded by various scientific foundations, involved data collection, processing and publishing. The data collected and processed is shared immediately among the members of the network, and two years after completion of fieldwork, the data is published for public use. A deeper analysis of this data reveals the cultural beliefs of the public in different and diverse cultures as in different countries under investigation.[10]

The public perception of facial recognition technology by law enforcement agencies and how they accept this technology is different in various cultures. Based on a recent online survey conducted among the internet-connected population in China, Germany, the United Kingdom, and the United States, the study finds that facial recognition technology enjoys the highest acceptance among general respondents in China, while acceptance is lowest in Germany, and the United Kingdom and the United States are in between.

A closer examination through the lens of an integrated technology acceptance model reveals interesting variations in the selected four countries based, among other factors, on socio-demographic characteristics and perceived consequences, usefulness, and reliability of facial recognition technology. While previous research has shown that facial recognition technology is an instrument for state surveillance and control, this study shows that surveillance and control are not foremost on the minds of citizens in China, Germany, the United Kingdom, and the United States, but notions of convenience and improved security.

In terms of people's general assessment of state-led public video documentation of the FRT, the latest World Values Survey[10] shows that the four selected countries differ: In China, 43% of participants believe that the government should "definitely" have the right "to keep people under video surveillance in public areas," compared with 26% in Germany, 35% in the United Kingdom, and 23% in the United States. It is worthy of note that the above survey also considered the diverse cultural influence of the population on the political structure in these countries which are China as a one-party socialist republic, Germany as a federal parliamentary republic, the UK as a parliamentary constitutional monarchy, and the USA as a presidential republic.[11]

Environmental Issues of Facial Recognition Technology

Face recognition technology by law enforcement agencies has been useful for policing services such as Stop and Identify, Arrest, and Identify, Investigate, and Identify, and Real-time Video Surveillance in suitable and conducive environments. Face verification allows identity pairing and profiling against a reference database. However, with FRT also comes many factors that may influence biometric performance and Face Image Quality (FIQ) regarding the scenery and environmental conditions.

There are many varying and unpredictable scenarios when using the FRT, as there is no control over the surroundings and weather conditions. Consequently, noise and performance degradation can be introduced by other people appearing in the background, different illumination conditions, different users' poses, and unstable and dynamic weather. All these factors of environmental influence and conditions result in quantifiable variability of face recognition performance. The environment where the authentication occurs is impossible to predict, as the light exposure depends on the camera's position and the daytime. Also, the facial image's background will not be uniform, as there can be many noise elements behind the users, including other people's faces.[12]

The ongoing discussion aims to assess the influence that the environment and the FRT camera's interaction have on the Face Image Quality (FIQ) and recognition performance. The quality of the analysis of the environmental impact on performing FRT is as reflected under the standard ISO\IEC 19794-5:2011[13] Information technology - Biometric data interchange formats - Part 5, Face image data and the guidelines described in the Technical Report[13] on Biometric sample quality. The quality metrics to assess the performance of the system in different conditions as guided by these ISO standards are brightness depending on the environment, background uniformity depending on the environment, background percentage uniformity, background type, and clutter, among others, as they relate to image illumination intensity, image brightness, Image contrast, etc.

Moreover, the environmental sustainability of the policing FRT is also of great concern because these FRT systems run on high computational power. The AI-driven FRT's lifecycle requires long-running training jobs, hyperparameter searches, inference jobs, and other costly model-fitting computations. They also require massive amounts of data that might be transmitted over the wire and require specialised hardware to process, store and operate effectively, especially large-scale AI systems. These activities come with a carbon cost that has a massive carbon footprint of carbon emission through energy or electricity consumption, natural resource degradation through equipment or hardware manufacturing, inefficient means of production and distribution of the FRT equipment to designated locations, and high cost of operation and maintenance of the FRT systems in public spaces.[14]

The new frameworks and thinking on Red AI (Artificial Intelligence) and Green AI seek to identify, define, advise, and advocate how FRT's production, distribution, operation, and waste management can be managed with little or no impact on the environment. According to a paper by Emma Strubell[15] and colleagues from the Red AI's perspective, an average American is responsible for about 36,000 tons of CO2 emissions annually. However, training and developing one machine translation model that uses a technique called neural architecture search was responsible for an estimated 626,000 tons of CO2.[16] The move towards the highly recommended Green AI has been encouraged in areas such as system reproducibility, increased system performance, increased deep learning understanding and transparency, democratisation of deep learning, and more collaboration and partnership. [16]

Legal Issues of Facial Recognition Technology

The FRT often utilises technology to match faces captured in near real-time video images. These faces are then matched against a watchlist of individuals provided by the police. Opponents of police use of FRT have argued that it threatens human rights, specifically the right to respect for private life.[17] In August 2020, the court of appeal found that the use of facial recognition technology by South Wales police had been unlawful.[18] This followed an unsuccessful judicial review application to the high court in 2019. The court of appeal found no clear guidance on using FRT and that South Wales police did not take reasonable steps to ensure the technology had no gender or racial bias. However, it did not outlaw the use of the technology, stating that the benefits could outweigh the human rights concerns.

In November 2020, following the judgment, the Surveillance Camera Commissioner issued an updated version of the best practice guidance on the use of facial recognition technology. In his foreword to this updated guidance, he argued that the police should be able to use facial recognition technology in "appropriate circumstances". However, he argued that "there remains opaqueness" regarding the legal framework governing its use.[19] There have been calls for a moratorium on the use of facial recognition technology by the police and other public agencies. In its 2019 report on the work of the biometrics commissioner and the forensic science regulator, the House of Commons Science and Technology Committee argued that the use of facial recognition technology should halt until a legislative framework has been introduced and there is better oversight of its use. In its response to the report, the Government argued there were already adequate legal protections in place concerning the use of facial recognition technology.[20]

As part of the effort to unravel the legal issues around the use of FRT, there has been a series of debates[20] among major advisory, legislative and regulatory bodies for a long time. Some of these questions have centred on whether thorough assessments have been made on internationally recommended guidelines and briefing notes on FRT, and what intended legislative and regulatory changes or amendments are to be made. For clarity, the most pressing of these questions bordering on legal issues are listed below:[21]

> 1. *Trend towards prohibiting/restricting FRT use*: There is an increasing trend towards banning or limiting the use of FRT, particularly in the US, where FRT is not permitted in law enforcement in various places (notably, in California). The EU has previously raised the possibility of a blanket ban on FRT use, although forthcoming EU regulation may seek only to restrict/regulate its use.

2. Bias and discrimination: It is becoming increasingly clear that, like humans, AI systems can cause and perpetuate bias and discrimination. System developers and the failure of AI systems to consider changing circumstances may intentionally or unintentionally introduce AI biases. In each case, such biases can lead to discrimination and unfair outcomes.

3. GDPR[22] and lawful processing: There are risks that the commercial uses of FRT may not meet GDPR requirements under Articles 6 and 9 of the GDPR[22] which deals with the use and processing of personal data via consent and legitimate interests by legal obligation, and if there is no conflict with "substantial public interest."

4. DPIA[38] / legitimate interest assessments: Under the GDPR, a Data Protection Impact Assessment ("DPIA") is required for high-risk processing before using or operating an FRT. An example is the UK Court of Appeal ruling of 2022 which held that the South Wales Police had unlawfully used FRT as, amongst other reasons, its DPIA was deficient.

5. Human rights issues: The use of FRT raises sensitive human rights considerations. For example, FRT can monitor individuals in public spaces without their knowledge or consent. This raises potential issues of the right to respect for privacy and family life, which can restrict a person's liberty and freedoms.

*6. **Public bodies using FRT***: Other public bodies besides law enforcement, like the academia, entertainment, HR agencies, retail sectors, etc., subject public bodies to additional legal obligations, exposing them to the risks of breaching the use of FRT (the "public sector equality duty" in the UK, for example).

*7. **FRT risks in recruitment***: FRT is increasingly used in HR/recruitment processes, particularly with the rise of video interviews (which has been accelerated by the Covid-19 pandemic) based on an analysis of various inaccurate data points and inherent biases that can lead to discrimination putting the employer in breach of its obligations, including under equalities legislation.

*8. **Explainability/transparency***: FRT involves the use of complex AI systems which may suffer from a lack of transparency or interpretability. Most FRT solutions use deep neural network algorithms, which are considered AI "black box" making it difficult to explain how the technology has reached a particular decision. The "explainability" of AI systems is already an essential component of ethical AI use, and we expect it will be reflected in the future regulation of AI.

*9. **Licensing and liability***: Organisations involved in the development, licensing, or use of FRT should ensure that their contracts specifically reflect the key risks relating to FRT that it has been appropriately developed and tested, that it is free of bias and that its use does not infringe third party IP. Equally, the licensor will want to ensure that the licensee remains liable for any unlawful use of the FRT e.g., any GDPR breaches.

Economic Issues of Facial Recognition Technology

The growing surveillance capitalism[21] which seeks to monetise surveillance technologies and solutions focusing majorly on sales and market size rather than societal service and needs, is a considerable concern. The consequent market size of FRT has increased on a global scale in recent years. The global facial recognition market size valued at USD 3.86 billion in 2020 is expected to reach USD 12.11 billion by 2028, according to a recent report by Grand View Research, Inc.[23]. The market is expected to expand at a CAGR of 15.4% from 2021 to 2028. Facial recognition as a contactless biometric solution is a critical factor contributing to the market growth. Contactless solutions enable easy deployment in consumer devices. It is also effortless and convenient to use, further contributing to rising adoption. [23] The growth projection is because of the versatility of FRT solutions enabled by AI, which are finding extensive use in various industries besides law enforcement, such as access control, attendance tracking, security, and others. These solutions include iris recognition, face recognition, speech recognition, and more. Facial recognition technology as a type of image recognition technology has gained wide acceptance over the years, leveraging connected or digital cameras to detect faces in the captured images and then quantifying the features of the image to match against the templates stored in a referenced database.[23]

As an indicative case study, the below figure of Asia Pacific's FRT project market size shows the trend of increase in market size from 2017 to 2028:

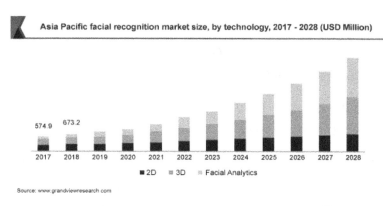

Source: www.grandviewresearch.com

Figure 7.1: Asia Pacific's FRT projects and market size[23]

Political Issues of Facial Recognition Technology

With the evolution of artificial intelligence in the last decade, particularly with the development of machine-learning algorithms, there has been significant progress in image recognition. As highlighted in the Politics of the Face.[24] some argued 'any system for representing the face tells us something about the society and historical moment that produces it'. In this sense, algorithmic facial recognition technologies must be understood as part of a long history of representational practices of the face, and both the roles these technologies perform and the forms they take can only be adequately understood in relationship to that history. This means that the human face should not be considered a universal or natural given but must instead be seen as the product of a specific social assemblage. [24]

According to a leading scientific paper published by Scientific Report[25] and backed by Stanford University on 25 November 2021, ubiquitous facial recognition technology can expose individuals' political orientation, as the faces of liberals and conservatives consistently differ. A facial recognition algorithm was applied to naturalistic images of 1,085,795 individuals to predict their political orientation by comparing their similarity to the faces of liberals, conservatives and others. Political orientation was correctly classified in 72% of liberal–conservative face pairs. Accuracy was similar across countries (the U.S., Canada, and the UK), environments (Facebook and dating websites), and when faces were compared across samples. Accuracy remained high (69%) even when controlling for age, gender, and ethnicity. Given the widespread use of facial recognition, these findings have critical implications for protecting privacy and civil liberties. [25]

However, there are pushbacks to using this technology and other forensic solutions based on privacy and civil liberties concerns. Many of the most passionate objections come from members of social groups who (rightly) fear that facial recognition technology merely reinforces and legitimises the gender, sexual, ethnic, and political biases that are endemic in our societies. There is also the fear that, as we see from China's ruthless exploitation of technology, it can lead to discrimination, exclusion, and perhaps even genocide.[26]

Ethical Issues of Facial Recognition Technology

Today, there are many challenges facing the FRT as used by law enforcement agencies worldwide. This book focuses on identifying and analysing the major challenges facing the ethical use of the policing FRT. Some of these challenges have garnered attention for some time, while others have been overlooked. The main goal is to contextualise and articulate the challenges so that stakeholders can better understand roles and responsibilities in deploying trustworthy and responsible FRTs in the Police department. Ultimately, trustworthy FRT policing solutions will only serve their purposes by ensuring effective collaboration between communities, academics, technology developers, police departments, and policymakers to confront and address these challenges.[27]

However, in a broader socio-technical sense, and as we will see, it may also require critically re-examining the role and value of police in society.[27] This evaluation of the ethical issues and benefits of policing FRT from both psychological and technological perspectives is to create a complementary trust relationship that would win public support and trust for its design, development, deployment, and operation. It adds to the discussion of the implementation and appeals to a layperson's judgment and trust through co-creation and co-implementation with the public.[28]

The main purpose of deploying ethical FRT policing in public and semi-public areas is to ultimately achieve and justify public trustworthiness by balancing the requirements of privacy and civil liberties with security and safety. The ethical analyses, as shown below, consider the arguments from proponents and opponents of FRT of the police department in society and whether the problems and challenges outweigh the value and benefits of the deployment of the system in society.[29] The ethical issues[27] considered are as below.

1. Racial bias and civil liberties

One of the most prominent objections to policing FRT, as found in media publications and academia, is that it leads to discriminatory treatment against people of colour or against economically disadvantaged areas or poor classes. This discriminatory treatment can result from a combination of two flaws in some predictive policing systems. First, the data used to predict high-risk places and people can have dubious origins. According to the differential selection theory, racial disparities in arrests are a function of racial discrimination by police in selecting whom to investigate and arrest.[26]

2. The standard of success or success metrics

Evaluating a data-driven FRT's accuracy, transparency, or fairness raises a fundamental question: What is the relevant standard of success? As well noted, human decision-makers are far from perfect for being influenced by racial bias. A familiar chorus among critics of predictive policing is that predictive policing systems will discriminate against people of colour. There is a need to ascertain what constitutes adequate and acceptable performance by the data-driven system such that a law enforcement agency is justified in implementing and operating it in their decision-making process. [27]

3. Explanation and transparency

The opacity of the design and implementation of predictive policing FRT, like many other algorithmic systems, has been criticised for their relative lack of transparency. A system is opaque and non-transparent when the input of a feature or some features cannot be understood or explained in the light of the output or the final prediction by the human designer, the decision-maker, and the affected person.

4. Accountability and community oversight

The appropriate mechanisms for holding law enforcement agencies accountable as a public institution are fundamental in this dispensation. The establishment and use of these accountability mechanisms foster public trust, enable the achievement of valuable institutional goals, and identify and address any problematic elements within the institution itself. But the value of accountability is also an intrinsic part of what constitutes a legitimate institution, particularly those, like law enforcement, that wield significant authority.

Impact Assessments - Balanced Assessment of The Impact of The FRT Application on Individuals, Society, Business, and Other Stakeholders.

People can unlock their smartphones with a glance and tag friends on social media based on face recognition. The biometric solution has changed and revolutionised authentication and authorisation forever. However, FRT, with its inherent benefits to society, comes with some drawbacks and issues with real-life occurrences like the killing of George Floyd by a US police in March 2020 and the UK's Court of Appeal's position on the police use of the technology to have violated human rights, data protection laws and equality laws.[30]

As debates continue among proponents and opponents of the use of the technology, below are analyses of FRTs as they impact individuals, society, businesses, and other stakeholders.

Impact Assessment Using Consequence Scanning Analysis

This analysis aims to perform consequence scanning (earlier discussed) on an AI-based FRT application, identifying intended and unintended consequences of the AI application from the point of view of all stakeholders and suggesting how negative consequences should be mitigated. This is as shown below:[31]

Name of AI Application:	Facial Recognition Technology (FRT)	Reference	6G7V0014 _2122_1F	Year	2021/ 22
Brief description of your selected application	This is an AI-based facial recognition tool to be deployed by the police department for law-and-order enforcement and management. The face recognition tool is a predictive policing tool driven by artificial intelligence's machine learning model, which is trained or supervised on types of human face recognition.				
Who are the stakeholders?	**Project Owner**: The Police Force **Secondary Project Owner**: Ministry (Agency) of Internal Affairs, The UK Government, and the Parliament **Target User(s)**: The populace/citizenry, criminals, immigrants **Beneficiaries**: Related government parastatals/agencies, the police personnel, international government				
What are the intended and unintended consequences of this AI application?	**Intended Consequences** 1. Capturing the picture of the human face 2. Tracking of people's location and movement 3. Efficient processing of personal data for better use 4. Storage of personal information and data 5. Efficient security and safety management				

Name of AI Application:	Facial Recognition Technology (FRT)	Reference	6G7V0014 _2122_1F	Year	2021/ 22
	Unintended Consequences 1. Abuse of information 2. Human and system errors **3.** System downtime				
What are the positive consequences of this AI application?	1. Finding missing people and identifying perpetrators 2. Protection against theft and criminal acts 3. Efficient security measures in banks and airports 4. Efficient retail and shopping. 5. Reduction of human touchpoints 6. Efficient tools for organising pictures and data 7. Efficient medical treatment and research				
What are the consequences we want to mitigate?	1. Threat to individual and societal privacy 2. Infringement of personal freedoms 3. Violation of personal rights 4. Creates data vulnerabilities 5. Fraudulent and criminal tools 6. Imperfect technology 8. Exploitation and manipulation of FRT				

Table 7.1: Consequence Scanning[31] and Analysis for Facial Recognition Technology

Harms Modelling (Foundations of Assessing Harm)

Harms Modelling[32] is a practice developed by Microsoft to help organisations expect potential harm and identify gaps in products and services that could expose people to risk. The analysis or modelling for the FRT is shown below.

The following contributing factors are examples for reference:

Contributing factor	Definition
Severity	How acutely could technology impact an individual or group's well-being?
Scale	How broadly could the impact on well-being be experienced across populations or groups?
Probability	How likely will the technology impact an individual or group's well-being?
Frequency	How often would an individual or group experience an impact on their well-being from the technology?

The categories and the potential overall harm are depicted as Low, Moderate or High.

▼ Low

■ Moderate

▲ High

Harms modelling - Harms Modelling Assessment and Analysis

CATEGORY	TYPE OF HARM	*Severity*	*Scale*	*Probability*	*Frequency*	POTENTIAL
Risk of Injuries	Physical or infrastructure damage	▽	▽	▽	▽	Low
	Emotional or psychological distress	▲	▲	▲	▲	High
Denial of consequential services	Opportunity loss	▲	▽	▽	▽	Moderate
	Economic loss	▲	▽	▽	▽	High
Infringement on human rights	Dignity loss	▲	▲	▲	▲	High
	Liberty loss	▲	▲	▲	▲	High
	Privacy loss	▲	▲	▲	▲	High
	Environmental impact	▲	▲	▲	▲	High
Erosion of social & democratic structures	Manipulation	▲	▲	▲	▲	High
	Social detriment	▲	▲	▲	▲	High

Table 7.2: Harms Modelling[32] Analysis for Facial Recognition Technology

Both the consequence scanning and harm modelling help to anticipate the risks involved in the design and rollout of an AI-based solution. As seen above, whilst the consequence scanning helped to have a deeper understanding of the stakeholders, the potential benefits (pros) and potential drawbacks (cons) of the deployment, the harm modelling gave a deeper understanding of severity, scope, scale, probability, and frequency of the potential harms that can affect the well-being of human and environment. Both tools are very good in proactively enabling, educating, and preparing the manufacturers, designers, developers, engineers, policymakers, and other stakeholders in the lifecycle of AI-based solutions as the solutions are deployed in society. Consequently, all stakeholders are aware, educated and prepared about the potential risks and to put measures in place to prevent, mitigate and resolve any attendant issues or problems that may arise.

Human-Centric Design in Building Trustworthy FRT Applications

As mentioned in the earlier section, ethicising AI applications and services, human-centric design and relevant best practices must factor in exponential changes and growth in the industry, especially with sophisticated facial recognition technologies. Organisations and stakeholders such as the citizens, policing agencies, government, legislators, regulatory agencies, businesses, manufacturers, and academia are urged to build on principles that have balanced the choice between social responsibility and market success.[33]

Major guiding principles as shared by a paper published by Microsoft in 2018[34] are Fairness, which is making FRT treat all people fairly; Transparency, which is for a manufacturer to be open and transparent about the capabilities and limitations of the technology; Accountability, which is having appropriate control in place to measure and manage functions that affect humans; Non-discrimination which is to prohibit unlawful discrimination; Notice and consent (specific, informed, and unambiguous) which makes manufacturers and owners provide notice and secure consent when they deploy facial recognition; and Lawful surveillance which provide safeguards for people's democratic freedoms in law enforcement surveillance operations.[34]

Below are the general thoughts on specific areas whereby FRT can be made more human-centric:

Human Centric Design (HCD)

The importance of Human Centric Design (HCD) in building trustworthy applications or technologies like facial recognition technology for law enforcement agencies cannot be over-emphasised. The HCD involves human perspectives, participation and engagement in the design, management, and engineering systems that develop solutions to problems. All stakeholders, including the designer, developer, end-user, etc., are engaged and made to participate in providing solutions through contextual observation, brainstorming, conceptualisation, modelling, development, implementation, and support of the solution's lifecycle. After the solution is implemented and integrated, community feedback is periodically collected for the upgrade and scaling of the solution.[33]

The HCD, as an interactive system development, is aimed at making the FRT applications and systems usable, useful, responsible, ethical, and trustworthy to the public and law enforcement agencies. The HCD processes also focus on the end users' tangible and intangible needs and requirements by applying human ergonomics, usability techniques and knowledge to promote human welfare and well-being, ultimately, user acceptance and satisfaction, sustainability, availability and accessibility in many ways to offset possible adverse effects. [34]

Participatory Research (PR)

The participatory research (PR) method encompasses research designs, methods, and frameworks that use systematic inquiry in direct collaboration with those affected by an issue being studied for action or change. The research method and tool can be conducted in a participatory, democratic manner in a way that values genuine and meaningful participation in the research process by actively and meaningfully engaging those who are not trained in research but belong to or represent the interests of the people who are the focus of the study which has the potential to create relevant, meaningful research findings translated to action.[35]

Consequence Scanning and Analysis

This is an Agile Practice for organisations to capture and analyse the potential consequences of their services and products on communities, people, and the planet. Consequence Scanning as an innovation tool allows innovators and organisations to mitigate or address potential harms or disasters before they happen in the conceptualisation, design, and implementation of FRT and other technology. In ensuring products and services align with ethical values and culture, consequence scanning helps to identify stakeholders, what are the intended and unintended consequences of the product or feature, what are the positive consequences to be focused on, and what are the consequences that are to be mitigated and addressed proactively.[31]. An example of consequence scanning for FRT is shown in the previous section of impact assessment.

Harms Modelling (Foundations of Assessing Harm)

Harms Modelling is a practice developed by Microsoft to help organisations anticipate potential harm and identify gaps in products and services that could expose people to risk. Harms modelling creates processes and means to proactively mitigate and address the identified harms. In designing AI or FRT to gain public trust, the conceptualisation, design, and implementation must reflect ethical principles that are deeply rooted in timeless values and culture. Therefore, it is crucial to know how digital technology could impact human rights.[32] An example of harm modelling for FRT is shown in the previous section of impact assessment.

Details of category-specific harms are described in the table below.

Ref	Category	Description
1	Risk of Injury	• **Physical injury** - Consider how technology could hurt people or create dangerous environments. • **Emotional or psychological injury** - Misused technology can lead to severe emotional and psychological distress.
2	Denial of Consequential Services	• **Opportunity loss** - Automated decisions could limit access to resources, services, and opportunities essential to well-being. • **Economic loss** - Automating decisions related to financial instruments, economic opportunity, and resources can amplify existing societal inequities and obstruct well-being
3	Infringement on Human Rights	• **Dignity loss** - Technology can influence how people perceive the world, and how they recognise, engage, and value one another. The

Ref	Category	Description
		exchange of honour and respect between people can be interfered with.
		• **Liberty loss** - Automation of legal, judicial, and social systems can reinforce biases and lead to detrimental consequences.
		• **Privacy loss** - Information generated by our use of technology can determine facts or make assumptions about someone without their knowledge.
		• **Environmental impact** - The environment can be impacted by every decision in a system or product life cycle, from the amount of cloud computing needed to retail packaging. Environmental changes can impact entire communities.
4	**Erosion of Social and Democratic Structures**	• **Manipulation** - The ability for technology to be used to create highly personalised and manipulative experiences can undermine an informed citizenry and trust in societal structures.
		• **Social detriment** - At scale, how technology impacts people shapes social and

Ref	Category	Description
		economic structures within communities. It can further ingrain elements that include or benefit some, at the exclusion of others.

Table 7.3: Harms Modelling[32] Covering Major Harms Categories

The EDI/B (Equality, Diversity, Inclusion and Belonging) Guidelines and Strategy

EDI/B (Equality, Diversity, Inclusion and Belonging) is a guideline for practices that ensure fair treatment and opportunity for all in society. The EDI/B guidelines aim to mitigate and eradicate prejudice and discrimination based on an individual or group of individual's protected characteristics when designing and implementing the FRT or other solutions.

These three qualities are as defined: *Equality* means fairness, which ensures that individuals, or groups of individuals, are not treated less favourably because of their protected characteristics and are empowered to get the tools they need to access the same, fair opportunities as their peers. *Diversity* is a practice that recognises, respects, and celebrates one another's differences. It creates environments with a wide range of backgrounds and mindsets, which allow for an empowered culture of creativity and innovation. *Inclusion* is a practice that creates environments where everyone feels welcome and valued. Whilst *belonging* is a practice that ensures individuals or groups feel like they belong, it also fosters a sense of being heard, seen, and recognised for their contributions. An inclusive environment enables the awareness of unconscious biases and provides ways to manage them.[36]

Data Privacy Impact Assessments (DPIAs) / Legitimate Interest Assessments

A DPIA[38] is a systematic and comprehensive way to analyse how data is processed and stored, helping organisations identify and minimise data protection risks. DPIA considers compliance risks, but also broader risks to the rights and freedoms of individuals, including the potential for any significant social or economic disadvantage. The focus of the DPIAs is on the potential for harm to individuals or society at large, whether it is physical, material, or non-material, and this is carried out by assessing the level of the likelihood and the severity of any impact on individuals.

For instance, the UK GDPR through the ICO[37] [38] highly recommends the DPIAs for the following projects and activities as they relate to technology solutions, e.g., the FRT:

- Use innovative technology like the FRT.
- Use profiling or special category data to decide on access to services.
- Profile individuals on a large scale.

- Process biometric data.

- Process genetic data.

- Match data or combine datasets from different sources.

- Collect personal data from a source other than the individual without providing them with a privacy notice ('invisible processing').

- Track individuals' location or behaviour.

- Profile children or target marketing or online services at them.

- Process data that might endanger the individual's physical health or safety in the event of a security breach.

The Environmental, Social and Governance Reporting

Organisations, both private and public enterprises, are rethinking and reimagining the metrics they used to define success well beyond profit and sales. This is in response to growing concerns among their employees, customers, investors, and impacted communities. Many firms are making themselves accountable for their Environmental, Social, and Governance (ESG) practices. Major investors once considered such measures "non-financial" but have now come to understand both related risks and opportunities, and they are demanding more related data. As a result, the amount of ESG information made available by rating agencies, technology firms, and auditing consulting firms has exploded, and efforts are ongoing to bring more coherence and consistency through concerted regulation and standards.[39]

AI for Social Good (AI4SG) and the Seven Essential Factors

The popularity of artificial intelligence for social good, AI4SG,[40] is growing in the technology industry and especially within the AI community. This framework can potentially solve ethical and social issues around AI-based solutions. The AI4SG initiatives are successful in selected projects in helping to reduce, mitigate or eradicate a significant moral issue. According to the work done, seven factors contribute to the successful design and deployment of socially good and responsible AI-based solutions. These are (1) falsifiability and incremental deployment; (2) safeguards against the manipulation of predictors; (3) receiver-contextualised intervention; (4) receiver-contextualised explanation and transparent purposes; (5) privacy protection and data subject consent; (6) situational fairness; and (7) human-friendly somatisation.[40]

Sustainable AI technology (Red AI Vs Green AI)

As mentioned earlier, the environmental sustainability of the policing FRT is also of great concern because these FRT systems run on high computational power. The AI-driven FRT's lifecycle requires long-running training jobs, hyperparameter searches, inference jobs, and other costly model-fitting computations. They also require massive amounts of data that might be transmitted over the wire and require specialised hardware to process, store and operate effectively, especially large-scale AI systems. The new thinking and framework on the Red AI (Artificial Intelligence) and Green AI seek to identify, define, advise, and advocate on how the production, distribution, operation, and waste management of FRT can be managed with little or no impact on the environment.[15 16]

Unified Theory of Acceptance and Use of Technology (UTAUT)

Technological advancement plays a vital role in changing and facilitating people's lives in various sociological and psychological areas, including communication, health, and the economy. The UTAUT2[41], which is the extended model, explains the objective and subjective factors that affect the acceptance and usage of Information and Communications Technology (ICT) like the FRT by end users or consumers. It also echoes that an individual's intention to accept and use technology is determined by seven factors which are significant predictors of acceptance and use of the technology: (i) performance expectancy, (ii) effort expectancy, (iii) facilitating conditions, (iv) social influence; (v) hedonic motivation (vi) price value; and (vii) habit. Moreover, the actual use of that technology is influenced by three major factors: (i) behavioural intention, (ii) facilitating conditions, and (iii) habit.[41]

Public Awareness and Empowerment (Education, Communication, Consultation)

To win public support and trust for the FRT and other solutions, the public needs to be empowered through appropriate and regular information sharing, education, consultation, and public communications. This is similar to an approach developed by the Biometrics Institute[41] using The Privacy Awareness Checklist (PAC). The checklist encourages governments and private organisations to incorporate privacy awareness and training. Also, in practice, it requires the maintenance of a robust privacy and data protection environment to discuss personal information processing and assess risks and threats. The Institute's Privacy and Policy Expert Group (PEG) updates the checklist to keep it current and communicate accordingly.[42]

Regulations, Public Oversight and Co-Creation

In building inclusive futures and protecting civil liberties in the design and implementation of ethical, legal, trusted, and inclusive digital identity services, there is a need to incorporate balanced and stringent regulations coupled with public oversight. Equally important is the institution of independent and impartial international multi-stakeholder platforms for sharing knowledge and information about biometrics-led projects, as these would promote the responsible and ethical use of biometrics through thought leadership and good-practice guidance.

It is also recommended that open standards of solution design and development should be put in place, such as the Open Standards Identity API (OSIA) of the Secure Identity Alliance that enables seamless connectivity between all components of the identity management ecosystem, which are independent of technology and solution architecture.[43] The engagement and participation of stakeholders should cut across the spectrum of public and private user groups such as government departments, financial institutions, airlines, civil associations, suppliers and academia.[42][43]

De-weaponisation of Shame, Blame and Guilt

Finally, in ensuring inclusive and fair treatment of all stakeholders in the ethical use and acceptance of FRT and other ICT solutions, we must guard against weaponising the three nags of shame, blame, and guilt against a group or individuals by shaming, blaming, and making them feel guilty because of their different views, belief, and culture. The problem arises when these responses are turned against a group or individuals as ways, tactics, and tools to demean and belittle conforming or compliance. They become weapons, capable of inflicting sociological and psychological wounds which often time create resentment, discord, and community breakdown.

If not managed, any of these negative actions can occur without thinking, as either a reaction when triggered or as subtle acts of manipulation. However, as individuals and society, we must learn and endeavour to use more constructive approaches and means of education, dialogue, regulation, empathy, and compromise in engendering change, compromise, and compliance. Ultimately, we should perform our roles for the highest good of others, driving and supporting the provision of fair, trusted and inclusive digital identity services necessary for sustainable, worldwide economic growth and prosperity with equal opportunity for all.[43][44]

REFLECTION: AI AND MORALITY (THE GOLDEN RULE)

Jesus[Q1] said, *"So, in everything, do to others what you would have them do to you, for this sums up the law and the prophets"*
(Matthew 7:12, New International Version)

Personal Note:

8

THE GOLDEN RULE FOR HUMANISING AI

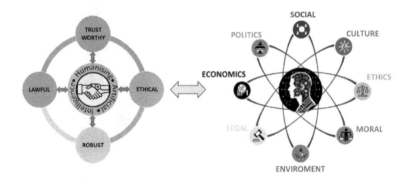

Figure 8.1: Democratising AI by Humanising AI – The HAI Model

Prioritising People Over Profit

Surveillance capitalism undercuts our privacy, autonomy, and democracy. The ongoing advancements of the digital revolution can be fascinating. But these advancements, with their bells, whistles, and lights, are blinding us to the reality that some tech giants are exploiting our data for profits. They are also mining our data to predict and shape our choices and engineer social behaviour, thereby undermining personal autonomy and eroding democracy in unprecedented ways.[1]

Balancing the forces of supply and demand and the interest of the big techs to make sales and profit is fast becoming daunting. The monetisation of surveillance treats the private human experience as the free raw material of behavioural data for profit-making resources and market share acquisition. The internet is expected to be a tool for empowerment, the democratisation of knowledge, and a platform for sharing economy. But with sole interest for profit and market share, it is becoming dedicated to a lucrative ecosystem in virtually every economic sector: from insurance to automobiles to health, education, and finance, to every product described as "smart" and every service described as "personalised."

On the political side, the politics of surveillance and censorship[2] related to FRT and AI-based systems have contributed to the erosion of privacy and freedom of expression, among others. Although privacy violations differ from country to country, the full extent of government surveillance in many regions remains unknown. However, disclosed data-gathering programmes hint at the architecture of AI-based systems lying beneath the surface of ostensibly democratic societies, and these are being used as political tools to identify, control and stifle opposing views in society.[23]

It is pertinent to point out that the efforts in humanising FRTs and other AI-driven solutions should involve the establishment of oversight by independent and public-trusted regulatory bodies and civil societies to facilitate public campaigns, open debates, and defend freedom of expression without fear of harm or persecution. Furthermore, these efforts must aim at preventing AI-based solutions from being used as vehicles to gain economic, political, and social dominance whilst using them as manipulative and coercive tools to gain control, engineer or engender unfair change to the moral, cultural, social, environmental, legal, and ethical fabric of the society.

Bridging The Human-Machine Gaps –
Democratising Artificial Intelligence

Innovations in AI and data management are widely perceived with scepticism and excitement. At an organisational level, the conceptualisation and operationalisation of AI applications with their inherent barriers, enablers, and drivers require in-depth and systematic humanisation strategies backed by strong leadership, governance, organisational culture, and processes. These encompass roles and responsibilities clearly defined, informed, engaged, and empowered to take ownership of standards, policies, practices, and regulatory compliance of the ethics of humanising AI solutions and innovations.

The bedrock of gaining public trust in the drives to humanise AI innovations and applications rests on robust ethics assurance, including human oversight with control and redress mechanisms that are established for incident, issue, and conflict resolutions. Moreover, the risk-based approach discussed in the HAI book helps practitioners and the public recognise and understand the various sociotechnical risk factors of how humans interact and relate with AI solutions in social, political, economic, cultural, moral, ethical, legal, and environmental domains.

Establishing tested human-centric and value-sensitive methodologies of humanising AI with multidisciplinary and multicultural engagements will go a long way to strengthen the trustworthiness standards of technology and legal and ethical requirements in making AI applications more humane and trustworthy. These are important as studies have shown that changing times and cultural trends influence humanisation standards and requirements regarding the design, development, deployment and decommissioning of AI applications.

Moreover, the theme and thrust of the HAI book is to further the frontiers of humanised AI innovations that are ethically robust and pragmatically applicable in all domains and situations. Relatively, it has provided practical strategies, how-tos and solutions that are human-centred and trustworthy to educate and discourage AI-based solutions from being used vehicles to gain economic, political, and social dominance to manipulate, coerce and engineer unfair change to the moral, cultural, social, environmental, legal, and ethical fabric of the society.

Mindless and unchecked innovations in AI applications will lead to humanitarian jeopardy and crises in the future. Our moral and ethical compass as a society should point towards upholding sound value systems that promote and institute acts of tolerance, open dialogue, education, diplomacy, effective regulation, compromise, collaboration and empathy in the design, deployment, and life cycle evolution of AI solutions and sufficient in preventing, mitigating, and resolving any consequent issues that may affect human life, values, well-being, autonomy and the planet.

REFLECTION: AI AND THE PLANET (ENVIRONMENT)

> *"As extreme weather events unfold with more frequency and intensity, AI can help communities around the world to better brace for climate disasters. AI-driven initiatives are targeting high-risk areas and feeding into local and national response plans."*
>
> - The UN Framework Convention on Climate Change.[29]

Personal Note:

9

TOOLKITS & RESOURCES
FOR HUMANISING AI
APPLICATIONS

This section highlights essential frameworks, toolkits, principles, oaths, manifestoes, codes of conduct, policy papers, white papers, statements, reports, and other resources in the global effort to humanise AI applications and data management.[5] The list below is not exhaustive as ethics and governance of humanising AI and Data management are still evolving in a dynamic landscape of AI innovations.

ETHICS FRAMEWORKS FOR AI AND DATA MANAGEMENT -

- **OECD Framework for the Classification of AI Systems: a tool for effective AI policies** by OECD *"To help policymakers, regulators, legislators, and others characterise AI systems deployed in specific contexts; the OECD has developed a user-friendly tool to evaluate AI systems from a policy perspective. It can apply to the widest range of AI systems across the following dimensions: People & Planet; Economic Context; Data & Input; AI model; and Task & Output. Each of the framework's dimensions has a subset of properties and attributes to define and assess policy implications and to guide an innovative and trustworthy approach to AI as outlined in the OECD AI Principles."* (https://www.oecd-ilibrary.org/science-and-technology/oecd-framework-for-the-classification-of-ai-systems_cb6d9eca-en)

- **Securing Machine Learning Algorithms** by European Union Agency for Cybersecurity (ENISA) *"Based on a systematic review of relevant literature on machine learning, in this report we provide a taxonomy for machine learning algorithms, highlighting core functionalities and critical stages. The report also presents a detailed analysis of threats targeting machine learning* systems. *Finally, we propose concrete and actionable security controls described in relevant literature and security frameworks and standards."*

(*https://www.enisa.europa.eu/publications/securing-machine-learning-algorithms*)

- **UK Data Ethics Framework** by UK gov, Includes principles, guidance, and a workbook to record decisions made (https://www.gov.uk/government/publications/data-ethics-framework)

- **An Ethical Framework for a Good AI Society: Opportunities, Risks, Principles, and Recommendations** by AI4People: *"We introduce the core opportunities and risks of AI for society; present a synthesis of five ethical principles that should undergird its development and adoption; and offer 20 concrete recommendations to assess, to develop, to incentivise, and to support good AI, which sometimes may be undertaken directly by national or supranational policy makers, while in others may be led by other stakeholders. If adopted, these recommendations would serve as a firm foundation for the establishment of a Good AI Society"* (*https://papers.ssrn.com/sol3/papers.cfm?abstract_id=3284141)*

- **Framework for Building AI Systems Responsibly** by Microsoft *"The Responsible AI Standard sets out our best thinking on how we will build AI systems to uphold these values and earn society's trust. It provides specific, actionable guidance for our teams that goes beyond the high-level principles that have dominated the AI landscape to date."* (*https://blogs.microsoft.com/on-the-*

issues/2022/06/21/microsofts-framework-for-building-ai-systems-responsibly)

- **Responsible AI in Consumer Enterprise** by Integrate.ai A framework to help organisations operationalise ethics, privacy, and security as they apply machine learning and artificial intelligence (https://www.integrate.ai/)

- **The FaithTech Playbook - Practicing Redemptive Technology by FaithTech Community** *"a way of building technology that redemptively changes the world while transforming those who build it. This belief has led the community to develop a redemptive way of building technology products."* (https://faithtech.com/the-faithtech-playbook/)

- **The Aletheia Framework** by Rolls Royce *"a toolkit that we believe creates a new global standard for the practical application of ethical AI. Follow the checks and balances within it, and organisations can be sure that their AI project is fair, trustworthy, and ethical. We are applying it in our business to accelerate our progress to industry 5.0."* (*https://www.Rolls-Royce.com/~/media/Files/R/Rolls-Royce/documents/stand-alone-pages/aletheia-framework-booklet-2020.pdf*)

LEGAL FRAMEWORK, CODE OF ETHICS, MANIFESTOES, AND PAPERS ON AI AND DATA MANAGEMENT

- **European Union AI Act,** "Regulation of the European parliament and of the council, laying down harmonised rules on artificial intelligence (Artificial intelligence act) and amending certain union legislative acts", April 2021.

https://eur-lex.europa.eu/legal-content/EN/TXT/?uri=CELEX:52021PC0206

- **EU Legislation in Progress**, "Artificial intelligence act", viewed January 8, 2024.
  https://www.europarl.europa.eu/RegData/etudes/BRIE/2021/698792/EPRS_BRI(2021)698792_EN.pdf

- **UK Artificial Intelligence Bill [HL]** – "A UK Parliament's Parliamentary Bills proposed to make provision for the regulation of Artificial Intelligence; and for connected purposes", November 22, 2023.
  https://bills.parliament.uk/bills/3519 - & - https://bills.parliament.uk/publications/53068/documents/4030

- **Summary presentation on the Act by the European Commission**, "Artificial Intelligence act", Future of Life Institute (FLI), viewed January 8, 2024.
  https://artificialintelligenceact.eu/the-act/

- **ACM Code of Ethics & Professional Conduct** – (https://ethics.acm.org/2018-code-draft-3/)

- **IEEE Code of Ethics** - (https://www.ieee.org/about/corporate/governance/p7-8.html)

- **Data Science Oath** by The National Academies of Science, Engineering, & Medicine (https://nap.nationalacademies.org/read/24886/chapter/7#32)

- **Ethical Codex for Data-Based Value Creation** by Swiss Alliance of Data-intensive Services

(https://www.academia.edu/39528443/Ethical_Codex _for_Data-_Based_Value_Creation)

- **Ethical Design Manifesto** (https://ind.ie/ethical-design/)
- **Manifesto for Data Practices** (https://datapractices.org/manifesto/)
- **The Programmer's Oath** (https://github.com/Widdershin/programmers-oath)
- **Governing Artificial Intelligence: Upholding human rights and dignity** by Mark Latonero (Data & Society) (https://datasociety.net/wp-content/uploads/2018/10/DataSociety_Governing _Artificial_Intelligence_Upholding_Human_Right s.pdf)
- **State of AI Ethics Report** by Montreal AI Ethics Institute (https://arxiv.org/ftp/arxiv/papers/2006/2006.14662. pdf)
- **Advancing AI ethics beyond compliance: From principles to practice** 2019 report by IBM (https://www.ibm.com/downloads/cas/J2LAYLOZ)
- **Operationalising AI Ethics Principles** by AI Ethics Lab (https://cacm.acm.org/magazines/2020/12/248788-operationalising-ai-ethics-principles/abstract)
- **AI Government Procurement Guidelines** by WEF (https://www.weforum.org/whitepapers/ai-

government-procurement-
guidelines?ref=blog.salesforceairesearch.com)

- **Statement on Artificial Intelligence, Robotics and
'Autonomous' Systems** - European Group on Ethics
in Science and New Technologies
(https://commission.europa.eu/research-and-
innovation_en)

ETHICS PRINCIPLES FOR AI AND DATA MANAGEMENT

- **UN Guiding Principles on Business and Human
Rights** by UN Human Rights Office of the High
Commission *Implementing the United Nations "Protect,
Respect and Remedy" Framework
(https://www.ohchr.org/sites/default/files/Documents/Publicati
ons/GuidingPrinciplesBusinessHR_EN.pdf)*

- **OECD AI Principles** *"The OECD AI Principles promote
the use of AI that is innovative and trustworthy and that respects
human rights and democratic values. Adopted in May 2019, they
set standards for AI that are practical and flexible enough to stand
the test of time." (https://oecd.ai/en/ai-principles)*

- **Linking Artificial Intelligence Principles** by Research
Centre for Brain-inspired Intelligence, Institute of
Automation, Chinese Academy of Sciences *"The following
table presents an analysis of different AI Principles worldwide
(currently 50 proposals) from the perspective of coarser topics,
which shows mainly on the consensus of various proposals. The
current LAIP engine enables us to list and compare between
different AI principle proposals at keywords, topic, and paragraph*

levels. Here we have the paper "Linking Artificial Intelligence
Principles" that gives more details on the design philosophy and
initial observations." ([https://www.linking-ai-principles.org]())

- **Draft AI Ethics Guidelines For Trustworthy AI** by
European Commission's High-Level Expert Group on
Artificial Intelligence (AI HLEG)
Includes a framework for Trustworthy AI , principles and
values, methods, and questions for assessing trustworthy AI.
([https://ec.europa.eu/futurium/en/node]())

- **Visualisation of AI and Human Rights** by Berkman
Klein Centre *"Our data visualisation presents thirty-two sets of*
principles side by side, enabling comparison between efforts from
governments, companies, advocacy groups, and multi-stakeholder
initiatives."
([https://cyber.harvard.edu/publication/2020/principled-ai]())

- **AI Ethics Guidelines Global Inventory** by Algorithm
Watch *"With our Algorithm Watch AI Ethics Guidelines*
Global Inventory, we started to map the landscape of these
frameworks." ([https://algorithmwatch.org/en/ai-ethics-guidelines-]()
[global-inventory]())

- **Principled Artificial Intelligence: Mapping**
Consensus in Ethical and Rights- based
Approaches to Principles for AI by Harvard *"Our*
desire for a way to compare these documents – and the individual
principles they contain – side by side, to assess them and identify
trends, and to uncover the hidden momentum in a fractured, global
conversation around the future of AI, resulted in this white paper
and the associated data visualisation."
([https://dash.harvard.edu/bitstream/handle/1/42160420/H]()

LS%20White%20Paper%20Final_v3.pdf?sequence=1&isAllowed=y)

ETHICS TOOLKITS FOR AI AND DATA MANAGEMENT

- **Algorithmic Impact Assessment Tool** by Canadian Government *"The tool is a questionnaire that determines the impact level of an automated decision-system. It is composed of 48 risk and 33 mitigation questions. Assessment scores are based on many factors, including systems design, algorithm, decision type, impact and data."*

  (*https://www.canada.ca/en/government/system/digital-government/digital-government-innovations/responsible-use-ai/algorithmic-impact-assessment.html*)

- **NASSCOM Responsible AI Resource Kit by** Indian Government *"The Responsible AI Resource Kit is the culmination of a joint collaboration between NASSCOM and leading industry partners to foster a responsible self-regulatory regime for AI-led enterprise in India. The Resource Kit comprises sector-agnostic technology and management tools and guidance for AI-led enterprises to grow and scale while prioritising user trust and safety above all."* (*https://indiaai.gov.in/responsible-ai/homepage*)

- **AI and data protection risk toolkit** by UK Government *"Our AI toolkit is designed to provide further practical support to organisations to reduce the risks to individuals' rights and freedoms caused by of their own AI systems."* (*https://ico.org.uk/for-organisations/uk-gdpr-guidance-and-*

resources/artificial-intelligence/guidance-on-ai-and-data-protection/ai-and-data-protection-risk-toolkit)

- **People + AI Research Guidebook** by Google *"A friendly, practical guide that lays out some best practices for creating useful, responsible AI applications."* (*https://pair.withgoogle.com*)

- **Model Card Toolkit** by Google *"The Model Card Toolkit (MCT) streamlines and automates generation of Model Cards, machine learning documents that provide context and transparency into a model's development and performance. Integrating the MCT into your ML pipeline enables the sharing model metadata and metrics with researchers, developers, reporters, and more."* (*https://github.com/tensorflow/model-card-toolkit*)

- **System Cards, a new resource for understanding how AI systems work** by Facebook *"This inaugural AI System Card outlines the AI models that comprise an AI system and can help enable a better understanding of how these systems operate based on an individual's history, preferences, settings, and more."* (*https://ai.facebook.com/tools/system-cards*)

- **Playing with AI Fairness: What-if Tool** by Google *"Google's new machine learning diagnostic tool lets users try on five different fairness"* (*https://pair-code.github.io/what-if-tool/ai-fairness.html*)

- **Ethics in Tech Toolkit for engineering and design practice by Santa Clara Univ. Markkula Centre** *"Each tool performs a different ethical function, and can be further customised for specific applications. Team/project leaders should reflect carefully on how each tool can best be used in their team or* *project settings."* (https://www.scu.edu/ethics-in-technology-practice/ethical-toolkit)

- **Responsible Innovation: A Best Practices Toolkit** by Microsoft *"This toolkit provides developers with a set of practices in development, for anticipating and addressing the potential negative impacts of technology on people."* (https://learn.microsoft.com/en-us/azure/architecture/guide/responsible-innovation/)

- **Responsible AI Toolbox** by Microsoft *"A suite of tools for a customised, end-to-end responsible AI experience."* (https://responsibleaitoolbox.ai)

- **Human-AI eXperience (HAX) Toolkit** by Microsoft *"The Guidelines for Human-AI Interaction provide best practices for how an AI system should interact with people. The HAX Workbook drives team alignment when planning for Guideline implementation. The HAX design patterns save you time by describing how to apply established solutions when implementing the Guidelines. The HAX Playbook helps you identify and plan for common interaction failure scenarios. You can browse Guidelines, design patterns, and many examples in the HAX Design Library."* (https://www.microsoft.com/en-us/haxtoolkit)

- **AI Fairness & Explainability 360** by IBM *Open source with case studies, code, and anti-bias algorithms, tutorials, demos & state-of-the-art explainability algorithms (Similar to explainable AI – XAI) (White paper)* (https://ethicstoolkit.ai)

- **Aequitas** by the University of Chicago Centre for Data Science and Public Policy *"The Bias Report is powered by Aequitas, an open-source bias audit toolkit for machine learning developers, analysts, and policymakers to audit machine* *learning models for discrimination and bias and make informed and equitable decisions around developing and deploying predictive risk-assessment tools." (http://aequitas.dssg.io)*

- **Design Ethically Toolkit** by Kat Zhou (IBM) *A library of exercises and resources to integrate ethical design into your practice.*
(https://www.designethically.com/toolkit?ref=blog.sales forceairesearch.com)

- **Algorithmic Accountability Policy Toolkit** - AI Now Institute *"The following toolkit should provide legal and policy advocates with a basic understanding of government use of algorithms including, a breakdown of key concepts and questions that may come up when engaging with this issue, an overview of existing research, and summaries of algorithmic systems currently used in government. This toolkit also includes resources for advocates interested in or currently engaged in work to uncover where algorithms are being used and to create transparency and accountability mechanisms."*
(https://ainowinstitute.org/aap-toolkit.pdf)

- **Lime** by the University of Washington *Open-source toolkit "explaining the predictions of any machine learning classifier."* (https://ainowinstitute.org/aap-toolkit.pdf)

- **PWC Responsible AI Toolkit** *"Our Responsible AI Toolkit is a suite of customisable frameworks, tools and processes designed to help you harness the power of AI in an ethical and responsible manner - from strategy through execution. With the Responsible AI toolkit, we'll tailor our solutions to address your organisation's unique business requirements and AI maturity."*

- **Algorithmic Equality Toolkit (AEKit)** by ACLU Washington *"The Algorithmic Equity Toolkit (AEKit for short) is a collection of four components designed to identify surveillance and decision-making technologies used by governments; make sense of how those technologies work; and pose questions about their impacts, effectiveness, and oversight."*

  (*https://www.aclu-wa.org/AEKit*)

- **The MSW@USC Diversity Toolkit: A Guide to Discussing Identity, Power, and Privilege**: *"This toolkit is meant for anyone who feels there is a lack of productive discourse around issues of diversity and the role of identity in social relationships, both on a micro (individual) and macro (communal) level."* (*https://msw.usc.edu/mswusc-blog/diversity-workshop-guide-to-discussing-identity-power-and-privilege/?ref=blog.salesforceairesearch.com*)

- **Pymetrics Audit AI** *"audit-AI is a tool to measure and mitigate the effects of discriminatory patterns in training data and the predictions made by machine learning algorithms trained for socially sensitive decision processes."*

  (*https://github.com/pymetrics/audit-ai*)

- **World Economic Forum's AI Board Toolkit** *"Empowering AI Leadership: An Oversight Toolkit for Boards of Directors. This resource for boards of directors comprises an introduction; 12 modules intended to align with traditional board committees, working groups and oversight concerns; and a glossary of artificial intelligence (AI) terms."*

  (*https://express.adobe.com/page/RsXNkZANwMLEf/?fbcli*

- **PROBAST: A tool to assess the quality, risk of bias and applicability of prediction model** *"A tool to assess quality, risk of bias and applicability of prediction model"* (https://www.probast.org/)

- **Dynamics of AI Principles** by AI Ethics Lab *"We decided to create the AI Principles Map to help understand the trends, common threads, and differences among many sets of principles published." (https://aiethicslab.com/big-picture)*

- **The Box** by AI Ethics Lab *"The Box is designed to help you visualise the ethical strengths and weaknesses of a technology. Once the weaknesses are identified, solutions can be created!" (https://aiethicslab.com/the-box)*

ETHICS CHECKLISTS FOR AI AND DATA MANAGEMENT

- **Trustworthy AI Assessment List** - *EU High-Level Expert Group on Artificial Intelligence* (https://ec.europa.eu/newsroom/dae/document.cfm?d oc_id=60440)

- **Deon** - *"Deon is a command line tool that allows you to easily add an ethics checklist to your data science projects. We support creating a new, standalone checklist file or appending a checklist to an existing analysis in many common formats." (https://deon.drivendata.org)*

- **Data Ethics Checklist** – *"a checklist for people who are working on data projects"*

(https://www.oreilly.com/radar/of-oaths-and-checklists/)

- **Ten Simple Rules for Responsible Big Data Research** - *"This is an open access article, free of all copyright, and may be freely reproduced, distributed, transmitted, modified, built upon, or otherwise used by anyone for any lawful purpose. The work is made available under the Creative Commons CC0 public domain dedication."*

  (https://journals.plos.org/ploscompbiol/article?id=10.1371/journal.pcbi.1005399)

MAIN NOTES

Quote Note

- Q1 - The Golden Rule for Humanising Artificial Intelligence - History & Society, "Jesus", Britannica, January 4, 2024.
- https://www.britannica.com/biography/Jesus/The-Jewish-religion-in-the-1st-century
- Q2 - Geoffrey Hinton, "The promise, risks of advanced AI", CBS Interview, October 8, 2023. https://www.cbsnews.com/news/geoffrey-hinton-ai-dangers-60-minutes-transcript/#:~:text=Geoffrey%20Hinton%3A%20We%20have%20a,going%20on%20in%20your%20brain
- Q3 - Alan Turing (English mathematician, computer scientist, logician, cryptanalyst, philosopher, and theoretical biologist), https://www.turing.org.uk/
- Q4 - History & Society, "Elon Musk - American Entrepreneur", Britannica, January 4, 2024. https://www.britannica.com/biography/Elon-Musk
- Q5 - Peter Diamandis, "My Thoughts on AI", July 21, 2023. https://mattersjournal.com/stories/what-the-biggest-minds-on-the-planet-are-saying-about-the-future-of-ai
- Q6 - Gray Scott (Futurist, Philosopher, Artist), https://www.grayscott.com/
- Q7 - Robert Williams, "First man wrongfully arrested because of facial recognition testifies as California weighs new bills", April 14, 2023. https://www.theguardian.com/us-news/2023/apr/27/california-police-facial-recognition-software
- Q8 - Chatham House Report, "Artificial Intelligence and International Affairs", June 14, 2018. https://www.chathamhouse.org/2018/06/artificial-intelligence-and-international-affairs/1-introduction-artificial-intelligence
- Q9 - "How AI helps combat climate change", The UN Framework Convention on Climate Change, November 3, 2023. https://news.un.org/en/story/2023/11/1143187

Forward

I. Managed by Google, Complies with IAB TCF. CMP ID: 300, "Greek Legends and Myths", April 20, 2023. https://www.greeklegendsandmyths.com/talos.html

II. Alex Shashkevich, "Stanford researcher examines earliest concepts of artificial intelligence, robots in ancient myths", February 28, 2019. https://news.stanford.edu/2019/02/28/ancient-myths-reveal-early-fantasies-artificial-life/

III. Chris Smith, et al., "The History of Artificial Intelligence" University of Washington, December 2006. https://courses.cs.washington.edu/courses/csep590/06au/projects/history-ai.pdf

IV. Stanford Encyclopedia of Philosophy, "The Turing Test", October 4, 2021. https://plato.stanford.edu/entries/turing-test/

V. Cambridge Dictionary, "Humanization, humanising, etc. ", Cambridge University Press & Assessment 2024. https://dictionary.cambridge.org/dictionary/english/humanization

Chapter 1

1. EU Science Hub, "The global race for AI", April 20. https://joint-research-centre.ec.europa.eu/jrc-mission-statement-work-programme/facts4eufuture/artificial-intelligence-european-perspective/global-race-ai_en - & - Gartner, "Gartner Hype Cycle - Interpreting technology hype", 2023. https://www.gartner.co.uk/en/methodologies/gartner-hype-cycle

2. Fabian Westerheide, "China – The First Artificial Intelligence Superpower", January 14, 2020. https://www.forbes.com/sites/cognitiveworld/2020/01/14/china-artificial-intelligence-superpower/?sh=675ce4e92f05

3. PwC's Global Artificial Intelligence Study: Exploiting the AI Revolution, "Sizing the prize", October 18, 2022. https://www.pwc.com/gx/en/issues/data-and-analytics/publications/artificial-intelligence-study.html

4. Chris Smith, et al., "The History of Artificial Intelligence" University of Washington, December 2006. https://courses.cs.washington.edu/courses/csep590/06au/projects/history-ai.pdf

5. European Parliament News, "What is artificial intelligence and how is it used?", June 20, 2023. https://www.europarl.europa.eu/news/en/headlines/society/20200827STO85804/what-is-artificial-intelligence-and-how-is-it-used

6. McKinsey Insights, "What is AI?", April 24, 2023. https://www.mckinsey.com/featured-insights/mckinsey-explainers/what-is-ai

7. Britannica, "What is intelligence, reasoning", April 11, 2021. https://www.britannica.com/technology/artificial-intelligence/The-Turing-test

8. Legal Interact, "Robot Lawyer to Represent Defendant in Court in World First", March 20, 2022. https://legalinteract.com/robot-lawyer/

9. "What is Artificial Intelligence in 2024? Types, Trends, and Future of it?", Great Learning Team, November 27, 2023. https://www.mygreatlearning.com/blog/what-is-artificial-intelligence/

10. Katherine Haan and Rob Watts, "Over 75% Of Consumers Are Concerned About Misinformation from Artificial Intelligence", Forbes, April 20, 2023. https://www.forbes.com/advisor/business/artificial-intelligence-consumer-sentiment/

11. Magali Gruet, "'That's Just Common Sense'. USC researchers find bias in up to 38.6% of 'facts' used by AI", USC Viterbi, School of Engineering, May 26, 2022. https://viterbischool.usc.edu/news/2022/05/thats-just-common-sense-usc-researchers-find-bias-in-up-to-38-6-of-facts-used-by-ai/

12. Jeff Hall, "Meta-Analysis Finds High Risk of Bias in 83 Percent of AI Neuroimaging Models for Psychiatric Diagnosis", March 17, 2023. https://www.diagnosticimaging.com/view/meta-analysis-high-risk-of-bias-83-percent-of-ai-neuroimaging-models-psychiatric-diagnosis

13. John Maszka, "Superpowers, Hyperpowers and Uberpowers", Jilin International Studies University in Changchun, China; International Journal of Research in Humanities and Social Studies, Volume 7, Issue 10, 2020

14. Lester Thurow, "Fortune Favors the Bold", Harper Business, 2005.

15. Aaron Mok, "What is AGI? How Artificial General Intelligence could make humans obsolete", Business Insider, May 27, 2023. https://www.businessinsider.com/what-is-agi-artificial-general-intelligence-explained-2023_5?r=US&IR=T

Chapter 2

1. Larry Chonko, "Ethical Theories", The University of Texas at Arlington, February 15, 2023. https://dsef.org/wp-content/uploads/2012/07/EthicalTheories.pdf

2. Ann Skeet, "What Is Business Ethics?", Markkula Center for Applied Ethics, October 19, 2022. https://www.scu.edu/ethics/focus-areas/business-ethics/

3. "Understanding artificial intelligence ethics and safety", Central Digital and Data Office and Office for Artificial Intelligence, June 10, 2019. https://www.gov.uk/guidance/understanding-artificial-intelligence-ethics-and-safety

4. European Union AI Act, "Regulation of the European parliament and of the council, laying down harmonised rules on artificial intelligence (Artificial intelligence

act) and amending certain union legislative acts", April, 2021. https://eur-lex.europa.eu/legal-content/EN/TXT/?uri=CELEX:52021PC0206 and ongoing updates here: (i) EU Legislation in Progress, "Artificial intelligence act", viewed January 8, 2024. https://www.europarl.europa.eu/RegData/etudes/BRIE/2021/698792/EPRS_BRI(2021)698792_EN.pdf (ii) Summary presentation on the Act by the European Commission, "Artificial Intelligence act", Future of Life Institute (FLI), viewed January 8, 2024. https://artificialintelligenceact.eu/the-act/

5. Jess Weatherbed, "European companies claim the EU's AI Act could 'jeopardise technological sovereignty'", June 30, 2023. https://www.theverge.com/2023/6/30/23779611/eu-ai-act-open-letter-artificial-intelligence-regulation-renault-siemens

6. This fundamental rights and algorithm impact assessment (FRAIA), "Assessing the Ethical and Legal Compliance of AI", OECD, April 5, 2023. https://oecd.ai/en/catalogue/tools/fundamental-rights-and-algorithms-impact-assessment-%28fraia%29

7. European Commission's AI HLEG, "High-level expert group on artificial intelligence" June 7, 2022. https://digital-strategy.ec.europa.eu/en/policies/expert-group-ai

8. European Commission, "Ethics Guidelines for Trustworthy AI" April 13, 2022. https://ec.europa.eu/futurium/en/ai-alliance-consultation/guidelines/1.html#Human%20agency

9. Central Digital & Data Office, "Guidance Data Ethics Framework", GOV.UK, April 14, 2022. https://www.intotheminds.com/blog/en/uk-data-ethics-framework-explained/

10. Quest Contributor, "How has the law been pushed aside in the age of AI?", University of Birmingham, April 14 2022. https://www.birmingham.ac.uk/research/quest/emerging-frontiers/ai-and-the-law.aspx

11. Rolls Royce, "The Aletheia framework," 2021. https://www.rolls-royce.com/sustainability/ethics-and-compliance/the-aletheia-framework.aspx

Chapter 3

1. Agence France-Presse, "AI Robots at UN Reckon They Could Run the World Better", VOA News, July 08, 2023. https://www.voanews.com/a/ai-robots-at-un-reckon-they-could-run-the-world-better-/7172680.html

2. European Union AI Act, "Regulation of the European parliament and of the council, laying down harmonised rules on artificial intelligence (Artificial intelligence act) and amending certain union legislative acts", 2021. https://eur-lex.europa.eu/legal-content/EN/TXT/?uri=CELEX:52021PC0206 and ongoing updates here: (i) EU Legislation in Progress, "Artificial intelligence act", viewed January 8, 2024. https://www.europarl.europa.eu/RegData/etudes/BRIE/2021/698792/EPRS_BRI(2021)698792_EN.pdf (ii) Summary presentation on the Act by the European Commission, "Artificial Intelligence act", Future of Life Institute (FLI), viewed January 8, 2024. https://artificialintelligenceact.eu/the-act/

3. Jacob Snow, "Amazon's Face Recognition Falsely Matched 28 Members of Congress with Mugshots, Technology & Civil Liberties Attorney", April 19, 2022. Amazon's Face Recognition Falsely Matched 28 Members of Congress with Mugshots | American Civil Liberties Union (aclu.org)

4. Jeffrey Vagle, "Cybersecurity and Moral Hazard", Stanford University, California, April 14, 2022. https://law.stanford.edu/publications/cybersecurity-and-moral-hazard/#:~:text=And%20so%20technology%20manufacturers%20face,the%20same%20to%20them%20regardless

5. Ameet Talwalkar, "AI in the 2020s Must Get Greener and Here's How The push for energy efficient "Green AI" requires new strategies", IEEE Spectrum, April 17, 2022. AI in the 2020s Must Get Greener—and Here's How - IEEE Spectrum
6. UK legal department, "Guidance Note on Legal Risk", 2015. https://assets.publishing.service.gov.uk/government/uploads/system/uploads/atta chment_data/file/736503/Legal_Risk_Guidance_-_Amended_July_2015.pdf
7. Edward Bridges, "England and Wales Court of Appeal (Civil Division) Decisions, The Appellant, Edward Bridges and The Interested Party, the Secretary of State for the Home Department, is responsible for policing nationwide", April 22, 2022. (Bridges, R (On the Application Of) v South Wales Police [2020] EWCA Civ 1058 (11 August 2020) (bailii.org)
8. PWC 2017-2022, "PwC's Global Artificial Intelligence Study: Exploiting the AI Revolution", https://www.pwc.com/gx/en/issues/data-and-analytics/publications/artificial-intelligence-study.html
9. Michal Kosinski, "Facial recognition technology can expose political orientation from naturalistic facial images", Nature Scientific Reports, April 27, 2022. Facial recognition technology can expose political orientation from naturalistic facial images | Scientific Reports (nature.com)
10. WVSA, "Social scientists studying changing values and their impact on social and political life", April 15, 2022. https://www.worldvaluessurvey.org/WVSContents.jsp
11. Genia Kostka, Léa Steinacker, Miriam Meckel2021, "Between security and convenience: Facial recognition technology in the eyes of citizens in China Germany and the United States", SAGE Journals, April 15, 2022. (Between security and convenience: Facial recognition technology in the eyes of citizens in China, Germany, the United Kingdom, and the United States - Genia Kostka, Léa Steinacker, Miriam Meckel, 2021 (sagepub.com)
12. Reid Blackman, "A Practical Guide to Building Ethical AI", Harvard Business Review Analytic Services, April 15, 2022. https://hbr.org/2020/10/a-practical-guide-to-building-ethical-ai
13. Kambria, "The 7 Most Pressing Ethical Issues in Artificial Intelligence", Kambria Accelerating Open Innovation, April 13, 2022. https://kambria.io/blog/the-7-most-pressing-ethical-issues-in-artificial-intelligence/
14. Channel4, "Deepfake Queen to deliver Channel 4's Alternative Christmas Message", Channel 4 UK, April 27, 2022. Deepfake Queen to deliver Channel 4's Alternative Christmas Message | Channel 4
15. Susannah Shattuck, "People don't trust AI. We need to change that", Towards Data Science, April 13, 2022. https://towardsdatascience.com/people-dont-trust-ai-we-need-to-change-that-d1de5a4a0021
16. Philip Meissner and Christoph Keding, "The Human Factor in AI-Based Decision-Making", MIT Sloan Management Review, April 13, 2022. https://sloanreview.mit.edu/article/the-human-factor-in-ai-based-decision-making/
17. Jeremy Davis, et al., "Five ethical challenges facing data-driven policing, AI and Ethics", April 27, 2022. Five ethical challenges facing data-driven policing (springer.com)
18. Real411 provides a platform for the public to report digital harms including disinformation, "Report online digital harms", January 16, 2023. https://www.real411.org/
19. "ChatGPT - Release Notes", OpenAI, August 4, 2023. https://help.openai.com/en/articles/6825453-chatgpt-release-notes - & - Introduction to Digital Humanism, Springer, December 21, 2023. https://link.springer.com/book/10.1007/978-3-031-45304-5
20. Ortiz, Sabrina, "What is Auto-GPT? Everything to know about the next powerful AI tool". ZDNET, April 16, 2023. https://www.zdnet.com/article/what-is-auto-gpt-everything-to-know-about-the-next-powerful-ai-tool/

Chapter 4

1. "First man wrongfully arrested because of facial recognition testifies as California weighs new bills", April 14, 2023. https://www.theguardian.com/us-news/2023/apr/27/california-police-facial-recognition-software
2. Bill Condie and Leigh Dayton, "Four AI technologies that could transform the way we live and work", Nature Index, December 9, 2020. https://www.nature.com/articles/d41586-020-03413-y
3. EU Digital Strategy, "Ethics guidelines for trustworthy AI", 2019. https://digital-strategy.ec.europa.eu/en/library/ethics-guidelines-trustworthy-ai
4. "Software Trustworthiness Best Practices", Industrial Internet Consortium, 2022. https://www.iiconsortium.org/pdf/Software_Trustworthiness_Best_Practices_Whitepaper_2020_03_23.pdf
5. Lisa Vaughn and Farrah Jacquez, "Participatory Research Methods – Choice Points in the Research Process", JPRM Scholastica, May 6, 2022. Participatory Research Methods – Choice Points in the Research Process | Published in Journal of Participatory Research Methods (scholasticahq.com)
6. Keeley Crockett, Femi Stevens and Tresor Lungu, "The Ethics and Governance of Artificial Intelligence - 6G7V0014/6G7V0035", Manchester Metropolitan University, May 6, 2022. https://www.mmu.ac.uk/course/ - & - Brown S, "Consequence Scanning – an agile practice for responsible innovators", Doteveryone, May 6, 2022. Consequence Scanning – an agile practice for responsible innovators – doteveryone
7. Keeley Crockett, Femi Stevens and Tresor Lungu, "The Ethics and Governance of Artificial Intelligence - 6G7V0014/6G7V0035", Manchester Metropolitan University, May 6, 2022. https://www.mmu.ac.uk/course/ - & - Microsoft Build, "Foundations of assessing harm", Microsoft, May 9, 2022. Harms modelling - Azure Application Architecture Guide | Microsoft Docs
8. Equality and Human Rights Commission, "Your rights under the Equality Act 2010", May 9, 2022. Your rights under the Equality Act 2010 | Equality and Human Rights Commission (equalityhumanrights.com)
9. Information Commissioner's Office, "Data protection impact assessments", May 10, 2022. Data protection impact assessments | ICO
10. MIT - Sloan School of Management, "Global Issue on ESG - World Economic Forum", May 10, 2022. Strategic Intelligence (weforum.org)
11. Luciano Floridi, et al., "How to Design AI for Social Good: Seven Essential Factors", Digital Ethics Lab, Oxford Internet Institute, University of Oxford, Oxford, UK and The Alan Turing Institute London UK, May 10, 2022. How to Design AI for Social Good: Seven Essential Factors | SpringerLink
12. Ameet Talwalkar, "AI in the 2020s Must Get Greener and Here's How The push for energy efficient "Green AI" requires new strategies", IEEE Spectrum, April 17, 2022. AI in the 2020s Must Get Greener—and Here's How - IEEE Spectrum
13. Alaa Momani, "The Unified Theory of Acceptance and Use of Technology: A New Approach in Technology Acceptance", International Journal of Sociotechnology and Knowledge Development and Research Gate, May 10, 2022. ((PDF) The Unified Theory of Acceptance and Use of Technology: A New Approach in Technology Acceptance (researchgate.net)
14. Biometrics Institute, "Privacy Awareness Checklist, Biometrics Institute", May 10, 2022. Responsible and Ethical use of Biometrics - Biometrics Institute
15. Becky Spelman, "The Weaponization of Shame, Blame and Guilt", May 10, 2022. The Weaponisation of Shame, Blame and Guilt | Private Therapy Clinic (theprivatetherapyclinic.co.uk)
16. Secure Identity Alliance, "Shaping the future of identity", May 10, 2022. SIA | Shaping the future of identity (secureidentityalliance.org)

Chapter 5

1. PEAs in Pods seeks to empower the Greater Manchester (GM) data science and artificial intelligence (AI) research communities, April 20, 2023. https://peasinpods.mmu.ac.uk/
2. Brown S, "Consequence Scanning – an agile practice for responsible innovators", Doteveryone, May 6, 2022. Consequence Scanning – an agile practice for responsible innovators – doteveryone
3. Microsoft Build, "Foundations of assessing harm", Microsoft, May 9, 2022. Harms modelling - Azure Application Architecture Guide | Microsoft Docs
4. European Union AI Act, "Regulation of the European parliament and of the council, laying down harmonised rules on artificial intelligence (Artificial intelligence act) and amending certain union legislative acts", 2021. https://eur-lex.europa.eu/legal-content/EN/TXT/?uri=CELEX:52021PC0206 and ongoing updates here: (i) EU Legislation in Progress, "Artificial intelligence act", viewed January 8, 2024. https://www.europarl.europa.eu/RegData/etudes/BRIE/2021/698792/EPRS_BRI(2021)698792_EN.pdf (ii) Summary presentation on the Act by the European Commission, "Artificial Intelligence act", Future of Life Institute (FLI), viewed January 8, 2024. https://artificialintelligenceact.eu/the-act/

Chapter 6

1. Likert scale, May 10, 2023. https://www.britannica.com/topic/Likert-Scale

Chapter 7

1. Laura Moy, "Facing injustice: how face recognition technology may increase the incidence of misidentifications and wrongful convictions", Georgetown University Law Center, December 1, 2021. https://ssrn.com/abstract=4101826
2. Khari Johnson, "How Wrongful Arrests Based on AI Derailed 3 Men's Lives", Wired, March 7, 2022. https://www.wired.com/story/wrongful-arrests-ai-derailed-3-mens-lives/
3. Eric Baker, "Defence Technical Information Center Thesis", Intelligence Systems Analyst, Texas Department of Public Safety BS, University of Texas, April 13, 2022. I've Got My AI on You: Artificial Intelligence in the Law Enforcement Domain (dtic.mil)
4. Baker, Eric M, "Rules around facial recognition and policing remain blurry", CNBC, April 14, 2022. I've Got My AI on You: Artificial Intelligence in the Law Enforcement Domain (dtic.mil)
5. Larry Hardesty, "Study finds gender and skin-type bias in commercial artificial-intelligence systems", MIT News Office Publication, February 11, 2018. https://news.mit.edu/2018/study-finds-gender-skin-type-bias-artificial-intelligence-systems-0212
6. Matthew Feeney and Rachel Chiu, "Facial Recognition Debate Lessons from Ukraine, Policy Commons", April 23, 2022. Facial Recognition Debate Lessons from Ukraine | Policy Commons
7. Martha Fors et al., "Validity of the Fitzpatrick Skin Phototype Classification in Ecuador", Journals, April 28, 2022. Validity of the Fitzpatrick Skin Phototype Classification in...: Advances in Skin & Wound Care (lww.com)
8. Tutorial Point, "Engineering Ethics - Moral Issues", Tutorial Points, April 16, 2022. Engineering Ethics - Moral Issues (tutorialspoint.com)

9. Daphne Leprince-Ringuet, "Police are investing in facial recognition and AI. Not everyone thinks that it's going well", MSN, April 14, 2022. Police are investing in facial recognition and AI. Not everyone thinks that it's going well (msn.com)

10. WVSA, "Social scientists studying changing values and their impact on social and political life", April 15, 2022. https://www.worldvaluessurvey.org/WVSContents.jsp

11. Genia Kostka, Léa Steinacker, Miriam Meckel2021, "Between security and convenience: Facial recognition technology in the eyes of citizens in China Germany and the United States", SAGE Journals, April 15, 2022. (Between security and convenience: Facial recognition technology in the eyes of citizens in China, Germany, the United Kingdom, and the United States - Genia Kostka, Léa Steinacker, Miriam Meckel, 2021 (sagepub.com)

12. Lunerti, et al., "Environmental Effects on Face Recognition in Smartphones", University of Kent, April 14, 2022. Environmental Effects on Face Recognition in Smartphones - Kent Academic Repository

13. ISO/IEC 19794-5:2011, "Information technology — Biometric data interchange formats — Part 5: Face image data", ISO, April 15, 2022. ISO - ISO/IEC 19794-5:2011 - Information technology — Biometric data interchange formats — Part 5: Face image data

14. Abhishek Gupta, "The Imperative for Sustainable AI Systems", The Gradient Publication, April 17, 2022. The Imperative for Sustainable AI Systems (thegradient.pub)

15. Emma Strubell et al., "Energy and Policy Considerations for Deep Learning in NLP", University of Massachusetts Amherst, April 14, 2022. Energy and Policy Considerations for Deep Learning in NLP – arXiv Vanity (arxiv-vanity.com)

16. Ameet Talwalkar, "AI in the 2020s Must Get Greener and Here's How The push for energy efficient "Green AI" requires new strategies", IEEE Spectrum, April 17, 2022. AI in the 2020s Must Get Greener—and Here's How - IEEE Spectrum

17. Edward Scott, "Facial recognition technology: police powers and the protection of privacy", UK Parliament – House of Lords Library, April 24, 2022. Facial recognition technology: police powers and the protection of privacy - House of Lords Library (parliament, UK)

18. Edward Bridges, "England and Wales Court of Appeal (Civil Division) Decisions, The Appellant, Edward Bridges and The Interested Party, the Secretary of State for the Home Department, is responsible for policing nationwide", April 22, 2022. (Bridges, R (On the Application Of) v South Wales Police [2020] EWCA Civ 1058 (11 August 2020) (bailii.org)

19. Gov.UK, "Surveillance Camera Commissioner releases guidance for police on use of Live Facial Recognition", GOV.UK, April 13, 2022. Surveillance Camera Commissioner releases guidance for police on the use of Live Facial Recognition - GOV.UK (www.gov.uk)

20. UK Parliament, "Work of the Biometrics Commissioner and the Forensic Science Regulator: Government Response to the Committee's Nineteenth Report of Session 2017-19", UK Parliament, April 14, 2022, Work of the Biometrics Commissioner and the Forensic Science Regulator: Government Response to the Committee's Nineteenth Report of Session 2017–19 - Science and Technology Committee - House of Commons (parliament, UK)

21. Simmons, "Top 10 issues for facial recognition technology", Simmons + Simmons, April 22, 2022. TechNotes – Top 10 issues for facial recognition technology | Simmons & Simmons (Simmons-simmons.com)

22. GDPR.EU, "Everything you need to know about GDPR compliance", December 24, 2023. https://gdpr.eu/compliance/

23. Grand View Research, "Facial Recognition Market Growth & Trends, Facial Recognition Market Worth $12.11 Billion By 2028, CAGR: 15.4%", Grand View Research, April 27, 2022. Facial Recognition Market Size Worth $12.1 Billion By 2028 (grandviewresearch.com)

24. Claudio Celis Buen, "The Face Revisited: Using Deleuze and Guattari to Explore the Politics of Algorithmic Face Recognition, Theory, Culture & Society", April 27,

2022. The Face Revisited: Using Deleuze and Guattari to Explore the Politics of Algorithmic Face Recognition (sagepub.com)

25. Michal Kosinski, "Facial recognition technology can expose political orientation from naturalistic facial images", Nature Scientific Reports, April 27, 2022. Facial recognition technology can expose political orientation from naturalistic facial images | Scientific Reports (nature.com)

26. John Naughton, "Can facial recognition technology really reveal political orientation?", The Guardian, April 29, 2022. Can facial recognition technology really reveal political orientation? |John Naughton|The Guardian

27. Jeremy Davis, et al., "Five ethical challenges facing data-driven policing, AI and Ethics", April 27, 2022. Five ethical challenges facing data-driven policing (springer.com)

28. Sebastian Weydner-Volkmann and Linus Feiten, "Trust in technology: interlocking trust concepts for privacy respecting video surveillance", Emerald Insight, May 5, 2022. Trust in technology: interlocking trust concepts for privacy respecting video surveillance | Emerald Insight

29. Danielle Ensign et al., "Runaway Feedback Loops in Predictive Policing, Proceedings of Machine Learning Research", May 6, 2022. Runaway Feedback Loops in Predictive Policing (mlr. press)

30. David Gargaro, "The pros and cons of facial recognition technology", ITPro, April 27, 2022. https://www.itpro.co.uk/security/privacy/356882/the-pros-and-cons-of-facial-recognition-technology

31. Brown S, "Consequence Scanning – an agile practice for responsible innovators", Doteveryone, May 6, 2022. Consequence Scanning – an agile practice for responsible innovators – doteveryone

32. Microsoft Build, "Foundations of assessing harm", Microsoft, May 9, 2022. Harms modelling - Azure Application Architecture Guide | Microsoft Docs

33. "Innovating for people: Handbook of human-centred design methods (2012)" LUMA Institute, LLC, May 10, 2021. https://www.worldcat.org/title/innovating-for-people-handbook-of-human-centered-design-methods/oclc/824525269

34. ISO 9241-210:2019 2019, "Ergonomics of human-system interaction — Part 210: Human-centred design for interactive systems", ISO, May 7, 2022. ISO - ISO 9241-210:2019 - Ergonomics of human-system interaction — Part 210: Human-centred design for interactive systems

35. Lisa Vaughn and Farrah Jacquez, "Participatory Research Methods – Choice Points in the Research Process", JPRM Scholastica, May 6, 2022. Participatory Research Methods – Choice Points in the Research Process | Published in Journal of Participatory Research Methods (scholasticahq.com)

36. Equality and Human Rights Commission, "Your rights under the Equality Act 2010", May 9, 2022. Your rights under the Equality Act 2010 | Equality and Human Rights Commission (equalityhumanrights.com)

37. Information Commissioner's Office, "Data protection impact assessments", May 10, 2022. Data protection impact assessments | ICO

38. Data Protection Impact Assessment (DPIA), "How to conduct a Data Protection Impact Assessment", December 24, 2023. https://gdpr.eu/data-protection-impact-assessment-template/

39. MIT - Sloan School of Management, "Global Issue on ESG - World Economic Forum", May 10, 2022. Strategic Intelligence (weforum.org)

40. Luciano Floridi et al., "How to Design AI for Social Good: Seven Essential Factors", Digital Ethics Lab, Oxford Internet Institute, University of Oxford, Oxford, UK and The Alan Turing Institute London UK, May 10, 2022. How to Design AI for Social Good: Seven Essential Factors | SpringerLink

41. Alaa Momani, "The Unified Theory of Acceptance and Use of Technology: A New Approach in Technology Acceptance", International Journal of Sociotechnology and Knowledge Development and Research Gate, May 10, 2022. ((PDF) The Unified Theory of Acceptance and Use of Technology: A New Approach in Technology Acceptance (researchgate.net)

42. Biometrics Institute, "Privacy Awareness Checklist, Biometrics Institute", May 10, 2022. Responsible and Ethical use of Biometrics - Biometrics Institute
43. Secure Identity Alliance, "Shaping the future of identity", May 10, 2022. SIA | Shaping the future of identity (secureidentityalliance.org)
44. Becky Spelman, "The Weaponization of Shame, Blame and Guilt", May 10, 2022. The Weaponisation of Shame, Blame and Guilt | Private Therapy Clinic (theprivatetherapyclinic.co.uk)

Chapters 8 & 9

1. John Laidler, "High tech is watching you", The Harvard Gazette, May 10, 2022. Harvard professor says surveillance capitalism is undermining democracy – Harvard Gazette
2. Arne Hintz, "The politics of surveillance policy: UK regulatory dynamics after Snowden", Cardiff School of Journalism, Media and Cultural Studies, May 10, 2022. The politics of surveillance policy: UK regulatory dynamics after Snowden | Internet Policy Review
3. Katitza Rodríguez, "The Politics of Surveillance", Sage Journal, May 10, 2022. The politics of surveillance (sagepub.com)
4. Luciano Floridi, et al., "How to Design AI for Social Good: Seven Essential Factors", Digital Ethics Lab, Oxford Internet Institute, University of Oxford, Oxford, UK and The Alan Turing Institute London UK, May 10, 2022. How to Design AI for Social Good: Seven Essential Factors | SpringerLink
5. Salesforce AI Research: Kathy Baxter, "Ethical AI frameworks, tool kits, principles, and certifications - Oh my!", September 15, 2022. https://blog.salesforceairesearch.com/frameworks-tool-kits-principles-and-oaths-oh-my/
6. **Image Credit**: https://thenounproject.com/icon/connection-robot-and-human-4116783/ - & - https://www.reddit.com/r/aitext2video/Centre
7. Exceptions: References and images are made from ethical public domains with respect of copyright. Kindly report any error or change, and amendments will be made accordingly.

Index